SHIPPING CONTAINER HOMES

The Complete Step-By-Step Beginner's Guide
to Building a Modern and Sustainable Shipping Container Home,
Including Plans, Designs, and Eco-Friendly Ideas

Daniel Lacewell

TABLE OF CONTENTS

Introduction 9

  Why Cargotecture? 10

    Pros of Getting a Shipping Container Home 10

    Cons of a Shipping Container Home 11

  Organization 12

    Units 13

Chapter 1: Building vs Buying 14

  Pros of Buying a Factory-Built Shipping Container Home 14

  Cons of Buying a Prefabricated Shipping Container Home 14

  Best Prefabricated Container Home Companies 15

  Managing Your Project 16

  Safety 17

Chapter 2: Meeting the Legal Requirements 18

  Legal Requirements in the US 19

  Legal Requirements in Canada 22

  Legal Requirements in the UK 23

  Legal Requirements in Australia 24

Chapter 3: Getting Started 26

  STEP 1: Determine Your Needs 26

  STEP 2: Create a Design 28

    Eco-Friendliness Rating 28

  STEP 3: Submit the Paperwork 29

  STEP 4: Buy the Container 29

    Pros of a New Shipping Container 29

    Cons of a New Shipping Container 30

    Used Shipping Container 30

    Buying Tips 31

    Transporting the Container 32

    Moving the Container on Your Property 33

Chapter 4: Tools and Equipment **34**

Excavation Equipment...34

Foundation Building Equipment 34

Cutting Tools..35

Welding Equipment...35

Insulation Spraying Gear 36

Carpentry Tools 36

Finishing Tools...36

Chapter 5: Building Procedures **37**

STEP 5: Prepare the Site...37

Choosing a Location 37

Marking Out Areas..38

STEP 6: Lay the Foundation..38

Types of Foundations for Container Homes 38

Ventilating the Foundation..39

STEP 7: Place, Clean, Cut, and Join...40

Cutting the Openings 40

Rust Treatment 41

Joining 41

Welding Procedure..42

Chapter 6: Reinforcing the Structure **43**

STEP 8: Weld the Supports...43

STEP 9: Installing Windows and Doors...43

Types of Windows...44

Types of Doors 45

STEP 10: Frame the Interior..45

Chapter 7: Making Your Home Comfortable... **46**

STEP 11: Install Insulation...46

Interior vs Exterior Insulation...47

Natural Types of Insulation...48

Artificial Insulation..48

STEP 12: Ventilation 50

Air Conditioning & Underfloor Heating 51

Chapter 8: Fixtures and Fittings 52

   STEP 13: Install Plumbing and Electrical Cables 52

   Plumbing 52

Chapter 9: Getting Connected 54

   Electrical Installation 54

      Grid Connected Homes 54

         Interior Wiring 55

         Exterior Wiring 55

         Grounding/Earthing 56

   Gas Supply 56

   Internet Connection 56

Chapter 10: Off-Grid Container Homes 58

   Electrical Installation 58

      Internal Wiring 58

   Solar Systems 59

   Gas Supply 59

   Energy Saving Tips 60

   Waste Management 61

   Connecting to the Internet 62

Chapter 11: Finishing Touches 63

   STEP 14: Install the Ceiling 63

   STEP 15: Build the Walls 63

   STEP 16: Prepare the Floor 64

      Other Flooring Options 65

   STEP 17: Installing the Roof 65

      Shed Roof 66

      Gable Roof 66

      Vegetative Roof 66

   Protecting from Rust 67

      Protection by Design 67

      Treatment 68

      Painting the Container 68

Chapter 12: Reefer Containers **69**

    Flooring 69

    Walls 70

Chapter 13: Example Projects **71**

    EXAMPLE 1: Single Unit Shipping Container Home 72

        Design Considerations 72

        Detailed Design 73

        Project Planning 74

        Project Materials and Tools 75

        Preparing the Site and Building the Foundation 76

        Window and Door Sections 77

        Electrical, Ventilation, and Plumbing Holes 78

        Building the Ceiling 78

        Framing the Interior 79

        Power Supply, Wiring, and Plumbing 80

        Insulating the Walls 80

        Building the Walls 80

        Building the Floor 82

        Approximate Project Cost 83

    EXAMPLE 2: Off-Grid Family Home 84

        Design Considerations 84

        Detailed Design 85

        Project Materials and Tools 86

        Preparing the Site and Building the Foundation (Contracted) 87

        Septic Tank Installation 88

        Joining, Cutting, and Framing 88

        Electrical Wiring (DIY and Contracted) 89

        Insulating (DIY) 89

        Installing the Ceiling (DIY) 89

        Building the Walls (DIY) 90

        Refurbishing the Floor (DIY) 90

        Building the Roof (DIY) 91

        Approximate Project Cost 92

EXAMPLE 3: Multi-Story Container Home 93

Design Considerations 93

Detailed Design 93

Project Materials and Tools 95

Initial Building Stages (Contracted and DIY) 95

Adjoining the Walls (Contracted) 95

Painting the Containers (DIY) 96

Making the Connections (Contracted and DIY) 96

Building the Green Roof (DIY) 97

Chapter 14: Other Design Ideas **99**

DESIGN 1: Container Home Blended with Wood 99

DESIGN 2: Horseshoe Shaped Container Home 101

DESIGN 3: Container Home with Mini Deck 102

DESIGN 4: Private Bedroom Container Home 103

DESIGN 5: Cross Stacked Container Home 105

DESIGN 6: Open Views Container Home 106

DESIGN 7: Decked Shipping Container Home 107

DESIGN 8: See-Saw Container Home 108

Chapter 15: Miscellaneous **110**

Space Saving Ideas 110

Home Automation 111

Tips 112

FAQ 113

Conclusion **116**

Top Shipping Container Home Mistakes to Avoid 117

Other Uses of Shipping Containers 118

References 121

INTRODUCTION

I only feel angry when I see waste. When I see people throwing away things we could use.
- Mother Teresa.

I am a cargotecture diehard. Of course, like every good thing, there is a story behind it. It's not a secret that our world has several environmental problems that threaten our existence. Since hurricane Katrina, I had been considering alternative living as a way of doing my part to create a sustainable world. The damage I witnessed also made me think about building resilience from disasters. It wasn't a natural realization that cargotecture was the answer. That awakening came after a close friend asked me to help with building a "zen studio" for a class that he was teaching. I had no idea what zen meant, but I knew I could rely on nature for inspiration.

I decided that a camping trip would surround me with the natural environment needed, and headed for the woods. To this day, I am still not sure whether it was a gut feeling or providence that led me to explore beyond my usual hiking route within the camp property. Nevertheless, it led to my eureka moment. Part of the forest was being used as a boneyard for decommissioned shipping containers. The rusty containers had taken over, and I could sense nature pleading with me to save it. I knew that I had found a new purpose and began to seek ways through which I could turn these discarded containers into something useful. I was cautious at first, and began slowly by meeting with other professionals in the industry. Soon, the architects and engineers I met had turned me into a true believer in shipping container homes. Inspired, I embarked on a journey to reuse shipping containers, and since then, I have converted several containers into functional and sustainable spaces.

They are popular today as a construction material with contemporary architects and design enthusiasts seeking to create sustainable alternative lifestyles. Some consider it the ultimate upcycling project, and it's easy to see why. I have owned my minimalist shipping container home for six years, and it has helped restore balance in my life by allowing me to connect with my loved ones. I constantly look forward to my weekend fishing trips in my shipping container home, which have become more enjoyable especially when I'm sitting on my patio overlooking the lake, roasting my catch.

In this book, I want to inspire you to consider a shipping container home by showing you the benefits for you and our environment. I will also guide you step-by-step in creating the shipping container home of your dreams based on my own experiences and the lessons that other builders have learned. If you are seeking a rewarding challenge that will help you live sustainably and make a positive impact on our climate crisis, then come along and follow the lessons that I will share with you.

Why Cargotecture?

Cargotecture is a term used to refer to construction using shipping containers as the major building component. When the world began to increase international trade, shipping containers emerged as an effective way to transport goods. I doubt that Malcolm McLean, their inventor, envisioned the challenges that their abundance would cause when he introduced them to the world. This is because like everything else, shipping containers have a designed functional life-cycle. Eventually, shipping containers are disposed of once they can no longer perform their function. Usually, they end up in shipyards, waiting to be recycled or reused. It is estimated that over nine million shipping containers lie unused across the world (IES, 2021). This is worrying because not only is it a waste of the resources initially used to make the containers, but recycling them is also costly. Melting a 40-foot container into metal blocks requires more than 8,000 kilo-Watt hours (kWh) of energy (Ataei, 2019). Intensive energy is also used for their manufacture and with thousands of containers manufactured each year, environmentalists are concerned by their burden on the environment because a lot of carbon dioxide is released into our atmosphere during their manufacture. Converting a shipping container into usable space is the best way to offset its carbon footprint.

Pros of Getting a Shipping Container Home

1. **It helps our planet:** Shipping container homes are good for the environment. Unlike the melt-to-recycle option, only 400 kWh of energy is needed to repurpose a standard single-unit shipping container into an alternative home or building. Comparing this with the energy used to melt the same container, the benefits are clear. Melting steel also releases carbon dioxide into the atmosphere. In the United States alone, emissions rose to nearly 1.8 billion metric tons for every kWh of electrical energy used each year (EIA, 2020). Other western countries' carbon emissions per kWh fall along similar lines. Repurposing a shipping container will help reduce the carbon footprint and contribute to saving our planet.

2. **Your home will last:** If done right, a shipping container home can last more than three decades before major structural repairs can be expected. It makes sense because the major component is incredibly strong and safe. Containers are engineered to carry large loads and endure harsh marine conditions. To make sure they don't fail in-service, shipping containers are heavily regulated and regularly inspected. A container used as a home will be subject to less adverse conditions than one carrying a heavy load across the sea, guaranteeing that you will enjoy your container home for many years. Even some doomsday preppers rely on shipping containers as the major structural element for their bunkers. For an ordinary container home though, you will need to perform significant structural changes if you want resilience from damages caused by natural disasters.

3. **It's easy to customize and scale:** Since shipping containers are modular by design; it is easy to stack them. In my opinion, this is the biggest advantage of shipping container homes. One of my last projects was a multi-story shipping container home where I was consulting for a friend who needed a container home built in a location dominated by duplex buildings. She wanted it to blend in to comply with the building codes. Structurally, the containers are designed to support loads up to 480,500 pounds (217,951 kilograms) on their corners castings. This gives a container the ability to carry another shipping container and several others, whereas in a traditional home, you would need to build a deck that can carry the upper rooms.

4. **You can take it anywhere:** One con of traditional homes is that you are stuck where you are. A shipping container home gives you the luxury of moving your home to anywhere you want, for as long as you have permission. Don't like your neighbors? Get a truck and take your container home to your wonderland. I moved my shipping container home from my backyard to the fishing lake to escape my noisy neighborhood. We will talk about the legalities of this a little bit later on, but the places you can take your beloved container home are endless. I have helped many folks haul their container homes to the most scenic places, and believe me, their lives have never been the same.

5. **It's affordable:** Shipping container homes start from as little as $10,000. The main reason is that building a shipping container home gives you options that are not available when constructing traditional houses. You can choose to buy a used shipping container and complete the entire build yourself. The flexibility of all these options allows anyone to save some bucks and own a home at a lower price than a traditional home. Of course, the costs of building a shipping container home are not the same for different regions, but it is generally considered one of the cheapest options for the benefits it offers. It can also be one of the fastest, and we all know that time is money. Because of its modular design, you can quickly construct your shipping container home and begin enjoying it in no time.

Cons of a Shipping Container Home

Some cons make shipping container homes less appealing. The main hurdle is getting a permit to build one, and the requirements differ geographically, so you must pay attention to the requirements in your area. Here are some additional cons that you should know before investing in a shipping container home.

1. **It's not easy to trace a container's history:** While an abandoned container can be purchased for a bargain, not all containers can be traced. From an environmental perspective, this makes it difficult for a prospective homeowner to be certain that the container is eco-friendly.

2. **You may need to reinforce the roof:** Shipping containers can be stacked because they can support loads at the corner of the roof (the castings), which is where the load is placed when you stack them. However, the top part of the roof itself is not strong and cannot support heavy loads. If you live in an area where heavy snow is frequent, reinforcements are needed to make sure that the roof does not cave in. In addition, off-grid container buildings may need to be fitted with solar panels, which also adds extra weight to the roof structure. The roof may need to be strengthened to support the weight of the panels. While simple designs, particularly single-unit container homes, can get away with roofs that are not reinforced, your requirements and environment will determine if you need to have the roof reinforced.

3. **They are heavy:** Usually, the container arrives as one giant piece of metal. It is not easy to move it around or make adjustments. This is why it is important that you choose the delivery of your container carefully, and schedule it after your foundations have been set.

4. **Insulation is a must:** Unless you live in a climate that is fair throughout the year, there is no compromise on insulation. An uninsulated container home can become a freezer during winter, and turn into a hot oven in the summer months. Even if air conditioning is available, installing insulation is necessary to save on electrical costs and avoid running your unit constantly.

5. **They are small:** There isn't much space available in a shipping container. Things that need to be considered include the space that will be taken up by insulation, electrical installations, and plumbing. However, with a little innovation, you will find that a shipping container home can be as com-

fortable as any other home. Building with several shipping containers is also a solution for people who value living space.

6. **Shortage of contractors:** The main reason people take the DIY route is that not many contractors are available to build a shipping container home compared to traditional lumber or brick houses. Building guidelines are not standard, and the building permits are approved on a case-by-case basis if they are applicable.

7. **They do not fit the normal aesthetic opinions:** I have had people call my homes nasty names. For some, the shape and the finish of a shipping container home is not aesthetically pleasing. In this regard, some local authorities have placed restrictions on where a shipping container home can be placed based on the visual appeal of the neighborhood. This is very common in Australia.

Despite all this, the pros outweigh the cons when we consider the environmental impact and the cost to build a home. The cons of shipping container homes can be solved, just as the saying goes, "where there is a will, there is a way." The projections are that the shipping container home market will continue to grow for years to come. The benefits are clear and explain their popularity among people who are passionate about sustainability and eco-friendliness. Personally, my life has changed and is more fulfilling and unique as a result of my shipping container home. I can assure you that building a shipping container home will do much more for you. You don't need to wait any longer.

Organization

Building a shipping container home is a detailed process that is similar to building a traditional home. The chapters in this book are structured to guide you through each stage, and you will find that the steps discussed will apply to the parts of the build that you will carry out as a DIYer. I have made an attempt to exclude the steps which a regular DIYer will need to contract or have no control over. The focus is the shell of the container structure, structural support, as well as making the home comfortable and safe for occupation. Although this guide will be more detailed in providing the steps of building a container home, building a shipping container home generally involves:

- Planning and consultation.
- Permit application.
- Purchasing the shipping container.
- Building the foundation.
- Modifying the shipping container.
- Building and insulating the ceiling and walls.
- Installing the doors, windows, and floor.
- Making the connections to utilities.
- Putting in the finishing touches.

We will begin by detailing the legal limitations of using shipping containers as building components, before proceeding to the materials available on the market today. Additionally, I will teach you how to select eco-friendly materials that will give your project a good eco-friendliness rating. Chapter 13 details three example projects intended to give you an idea of your responsibilities and the costs associated with different styles of shipping container homes. The costs of adding furniture and storage are beyond the scope of this book.

Of course, each conversion project is different, and complex builds will require more elaborate steps. When reference is made to a simple build, this will mean a single unit shipping container, while complex builds refer to any building that uses more than one shipping container. The steps presented in this book will be based on the general steps required to build a container home, and some steps will be expanded on to give more detail.

Chapter 14 will also illustrate some additional design ideas for shipping container homes.

Units

The information presented in this guide is intended for individuals who want to build their container homes in the United States, The United Kingdom, Canada, and Australia. Only important dimensions and measurements are presented in both imperial and metric units. If the units are not expressed in the units you are familiar with, please use the following conversions:

- **length:** one foot (ft) = 30.48 centimeters (cm); one inch (in) = 2.54 cm
- **area:** one square foot (sq ft) = 0.092 square meters (sq m)

CHAPTER 1
BUILDING VS BUYING

There are two ways to own a shipping container home. You can choose to build the shipping container home yourself or order a completed house. Factory made container homes are normally referred to as prefabricated shipping container homes. This market is growing because although people are convinced that shipping containers are the ideal structure for building alternative homes, not everyone has the skills to convert the containers. The lack of experienced contractors relative to traditional building has also influenced the decision to buy prefabricated homes. When cargotecture started, there were few players in the industry and the absence of standards made it a niche market. Regardless of the option you choose, there are pros and cons for each, and you will need to consider them before making a commitment. Your budget and the time you are willing to invest in building the house can help you decide.

Pros of Buying a Factory-Built Shipping Container Home

No hassle: The factory does everything for you. Some manufacturers even have in-house designers that can guide you through the design process to help you realize your dream. The factory also handles the inspections and consults the local authority on your behalf to determine which building codes to follow, so you do not need to apply for a permit. A structural engineer will visit your land to determine the type of foundation you will need so that the appropriate steps affecting the build are taken.

Shorter lead times: We all know that DIY jobs have a risk of delays, under budgeting, and frequent back and forths to fix any oversights. Prefabricated shipping container homes are guaranteed to be delivered within the specified timeframe. If you are in a hurry to get your house, purchasing a ready-made or ordering a custom container home is a quick and convenient option.

Documentation: The production process and the standards used are documented. When you want to extend using a different contractor, the documentation will help with the specifications so that the extension is of the same standard.

Cons of Buying a Prefabricated Shipping Container Home

Limited expertise: Compared to contractors available for traditional housing options, few companies offer prefabricated shipping container homes. If you live in an area where shipping container homes are still a new thing, you may struggle to find a local manufacturer. This will complicate activities like site assessments, foundation building, and the permit application process. The cost to transport a completed home will also be higher because manufacturers charge delivery based on distance. Plus, some companies only deliver within the states that their factories are located, and you might struggle to find a suitable manufacturer who provides the service locally. This increases the cost of the entire process.

Cost: It's more expensive to buy a prefabricated home than to build a container home yourself. Since prefabricated homes are heavier, they will cost more to transport. The cost to transport will also increase if the home has fixtures such as cabinets installed because they need to be handled delicately. One of the leading manufacturers of prefabricated homes is Honomobo. They are based in Canada and charge around $13,500 to transport the completed home, while the delivery is included in the purchase price if the house is built on-site by the same company. If you decide to order a prefabricated shipping container home, expect to pay for additional costs because manufacturers add overheads to the final purchase price that they may not necessarily incur if they build the home on-site.

Best Prefabricated Container Home Companies

Compared to buying a regular house, there aren't many companies available to supply a prefabricated shipping container home. Some manufacturers sell in the states where their factories are located, and I have prepared a list of the most reputable companies you can try. The list is not exhaustive, and neither is it an endorsement of the companies. Do some digging before you make a purchase, and check if the manufacturer's designs consider your local authority's requirements.

According to Prefab Review (2019), Honomobo is regarded as the leading manufacturer, and delivers shipping container homes throughout the Northwestern United States and Canada. They offer an extensive range of pre-designed models that can be customized to add extra features such as a garage. The average cost for a home is between $400 and $600 per sq ft without the land costs. Currently, eight models are available for purchase.

Backcountry Containers offers custom homes at a reasonable cost, although their services are only available in Texas and are limited to manufacture of the shell with utilities such as plumbing and electrical wiring included. The average cost is $400 excluding the land costs and site preparation costs.

Cargotecture is one of the few companies that manufactures container homes for the global market. The homes are shipped from the United States ready for occupation and will need to be connected to the utilities after attaching to the foundation. Only six models are available, but there are options to customize the house, including a green roof option. Expect to pay between $250 and $400 per sq ft.

If you are based in Australia, you can order from companies such as Studio Edwards, Spark Homes, Mipod Container Homes and Craig Dinte Architects. You will be able to find at least one manufacturer that services your state according to the state and local authority laws, usually at a cheaper cost compared to building a traditional home. The companies provide a full service including interior design and connecting to the main utility service. Single unit container homes can be delivered within a month after placing an order depending on your location.

In the UK, Turner Works, Inbox Projects, Nortons Cabins, and Mac Container Company are the popular manufacturers of container homes. The latter is regarded as the best in the country, and the options are flexible. The homes come with a warranty and a superior fire rating. You can easily customize the designs to suit your needs. If you are pressed on time, ordering from any of these companies is a great compromise.

Managing Your Project

If you decide to build your container home instead of purchasing a completed home, project management skills will benefit you greatly. While shipping container homes are relatively affordable, you still need to plan your time and money wisely. Poor planning will lead to poor results or an unfinished house. One tool that has been useful in managing my projects is a container home project management tool created by Discover Containers. It is sold for a reasonable price and can be customized to suit your needs. Fortunately, the internet is rich with handy project management templates that you can download to your computer and edit to suit your needs, and there is a lot of free stuff to choose from. You can always develop a planning tool that has Ghant charts if you want to manage your project like a pro. They will be useful to develop a schedule to guide you through the start and endpoints of each stage. Microsoft Excel or Projects are also options, and you may already have access to these applications if you own a computer.

On average, DIY-built single-unit container homes should take less than six months to complete under normal circumstances. However, depending on the size of your build, and the legal processes in your region, a shipping container home can take between three months and one year to build. I use concepts I learned from project management to develop the bigger picture of my build before breaking them down into elaborate steps. Managing the conversion project consists of the following activities.

Planning: Take around four days to allocate the required finances. Buying the shipping container itself is not costly, but usually requires full payment at the time of purchase, and compared to an ordinary home, the funding options are limited because banks are not keen on financing non-traditional homes. The challenge with container homes is that they are a niche market, and some state and local authorities still consider container homes as mobile homes. This makes financing container homes difficult. You can take a personal loan that uses credit-scoring instead of collateral to fund small shipping container homes. If cash is available, you can finance your home at once, or use an incremental-housing approach to fund each stage of the project.

If you have another home, a home equity loan can also help you finance your project. Despite the higher interest rates compared to getting a mortgage, you can get around two-thirds of your current home's value to finance the build, which can be paid off over time. Banks and financial institutions prefer to use this method to fund shipping container homes because their risk is reduced. In case of default, they will simply sell off the primary home to service the loan.

Purchasing a custom or pre-manufactured container home from manufacturers can get you the home you want if you are short on cash because some companies offer to finance customers. This is a great option if you do not want to complete the build yourself. Of course, there is no fun in that because you will not be involved in the building process, but it is worth considering if you do not have the DIY skills or the cash to complete a project. You can search for prefab container home manufacturers in your area to check out what they have to offer. One manufacturer that provides financing options is Cepods, with financing available for both commercial and residential container houses in the United States. In Canada, Honomobo is among the manufacturers that has a relationship with lenders, providing you with access to mortgage loans. Unfortunately not many manufacturers offer financing options. If you want to purchase a prefab shipping container home using a financed option, try discussing it with the manufacturer in your region.

The rise of social media and content-sharing platforms has also opened up opportunities for sponsorships and income generation through ads. If you have the skills, a decent number of followers, and a good personality, you can approach companies that make products related to shipping container homes and reach a sponsorship agreement. The money or freebies you receive will get you the home you have always wanted, and your sponsors might make a profit from advertising through you.

Map the Road Ahead: Once you know how you are going to finance the project, gather information and audit the location where you are going to build the home. Conducting your site assessment and selecting the materials suitable for your environment should take an additional five days. Information that needs to be gathered includes the local laws, available contractors, and structural engineers. Make a list of at least three professionals and choose the best one after factoring in their previous experience and cost of services. If you do not own the land already, you have to purchase the land before proceeding to the next stages of the ideation phase.

Finalize the Design and Apply for Approval: At least two months should be spent finalizing the design and preparing the paperwork that will be submitted for approval. Service delivery varies by location, and it might take you several weeks before your local authority approves the plans. It can also be a back and forth process because several versions of the plans are usually developed before the final go-ahead is issued. In areas that have a considerable number of shipping container homes already built, approval can be issued within a couple of weeks, but complex builds might take as long as 12 weeks for approval to be granted.

Site Preparation: Off-grid or remote builds should be dedicated enough time to prepare the site before the foundation can be built. Typically, up to six days are required to clear the land and remove any obstacles in the path of the delivery truck. The foundation can also take a minimum of five days to be completed. You also need to allocate extra time for curing if a concrete slab is used. Depending on the type of concrete used, you may need to wait between one and three weeks for the concrete to fully cure. Concrete needs water to gain strength and this should be poured on the surface over three weeks. Do not load the foundation before it has properly cured. The concrete will not gain the full strength required to support a heavy structure.

Placing and Working on the Containers: After delivery, the building process can last up to nine weeks. Activities include cutting, framing, insulating, and connecting the utilities.

Safety

Before you start, take some time to think about how you will ensure a safe working environment for yourself and your contractors. Tools allow you to complete work faster and save on labor costs, but operating them can be dangerous. In construction and related industries that use power tools, regulations such as the Provision and Use of Work Equipment Regulations (PUWER) provide legal frameworks that compel the observation of safe work practices.

Personal protective clothing is compulsory in regulated environments for a good reason. While you may not have the same regulations as an individual working in their own home, wearing protective clothing and using protective equipment will prevent you from getting injured. Besides, if you get injured, you may not be able to enjoy the home you intend to build.

Make sure that you read the manufacturer's instructions of the tools you intend to use. Do not use the wrong tool for the job and always know the limitations of the tools you plan to use. Your work area must be free from obstacles that can cause you to trip over, and cables must be clear of the walking path. I recommend browsing the internet to learn about how you can ensure a safe working environment. You can use the information to develop a simple safety plan to reduce the potential hazards during your DIY build.

CHAPTER 2
MEETING THE LEGAL REQUIREMENTS

The popularity of shipping container homes has led state and local authorities to develop building codes and related regulations to ensure safety and compatibility with existing infrastructure. There are several reasons for this. Firstly, shipping containers are heavy. The foundation must be compatible with the soil-bearing capabilities to reduce the risks of structural failure. For example, a standard 40 ft (12m) shipping container weighs between 8,340 and 9,260 lbs (3,800 - 4,200 kgs) (Bison Jacks, 2021). This is a heavy load that affects several things including the type of roads that must be used to deliver the containers. Checking on the weight restrictions of the route your shipping container will take before reaching your construction site is important. You want to avoid the disappointment of buying something you won't be able to place where you want it.

Usually, a heavy truck is needed to haul the shipping container to the site. I have seen some people use their trucks and special trailers to move their containers. While it's a cheap option, it is not the best because normal passenger trucks are not designed to pull such heavy and long loads. Besides, you will need to hire a suitable trailer, which may be difficult to find. You will also face difficulty with positioning the container precisely using this approach. Only haul the container yourself if you have the right equipment and legal clearance to do so.

Other than this, there are several reasons you should consider the building codes and requirements in your area. Although it will be up to you to get location-specific requirements, I have listed some important requirements that you need to know. The rule of thumb is that unzoned locations do not require a building permit to build a shipping container home. These are usually off-grid and remote areas that do not fall under the jurisdiction of a city council.

Legal Requirements in the US

The United States has an extensive list of requirements that guide the regulations. In 2019 the ICC published new guidelines for using intermodal shipping containers as homes made under the International Building Code (IBC), particularly Section 3114. Almost every state conforms to the requirements set out in the IBC, and there is a high likelihood that your local council adopts the same guidelines. The IBC also specifies the subsequent compliance criteria of shipping container conversions to the International Mechanical Code, International Plumbing Code, National Fire Protection standards, and the National Electric Code. In addition to these codes, many cities will have their own local authority codes, which may or may not be in favor of utilizing a shipping container home. For example, while the IBC generally permits container houses, places such as Atlanta only permit container houses below 750 sq ft behind the main home if they are intended for permanent use and are equipped with a kitchen. Unless otherwise specified, we will refer to the IBC's guidelines on the example projects throughout the book because they are more detailed than other regulations but you should always do your due diligence and research the codes for your local area.

Zoning Laws

With the exception of Houston, major cities across the country have zoning laws in place that govern where you can build a shipping container home. In Houston, the laws do not address land utilization. Instead, codes that specify property subdivision are enforced. In states that have zoning laws, the categories are based on type of activity. You need to specify whether you are building a commercial container structure or a residential unit to get a building permit. The major consideration is whether the area is classified as a commercial or residential zone. This information is available at the local authority in your state.

Friendly Shipping Container Home States

Texas: The state of Texas is ideal for shipping container conversion enthusiasts. Most of my projects were in Texas, because the state is less regulatory compared to the rest of the country. Of course the big cities might be the outliers, so try and locate your shipping container home in the suburban parts of smaller cities and rural areas. The turnaround time for getting a building permit in Texas is also remarkable, and this is why it tops the list as a friendly state.

Louisiana: Cato Institute ranked this state first on the land freedom index in the United States for a reason. Its regulatory climate is the most favorable because the zoning laws are not stringent. There is little regulation to the type of structures you are allowed to build on land that you own, and this should excite anyone looking to build a container home in the state of Louisiana.

Oregon: No state is more popular with the off-grid community than Oregon. It's considered the leading state on being progressive to alternative building and off-grid houses. It's 'live and let live' mantra encourages eco-friendly buildings, and this makes it a good place to test if living off-grid is for you.

Construction Documents

Before you can start building, most state laws require that at least the following details be provided.

- Verified details of container specifications, manufacturer or manufacturer's identification number.
- Date of manufacture.
- Container weight limitations.
- Stacking load (maximum allowable).
- Container maintenance examination dates. The building officer can approve the removal of data plates or any identifying information before repurposing if you are not keen on keeping the tags displayed on your home. Just be sure to have the records somewhere for your use, in case you need to make alterations at a later stage.

Floor Regulations

Naturally, the container floors decay over time as a result of exposure to the elements of predators such as termites, especially if they are left untreated. If you chose to remain with the floor the container is shipped with, then the treatment of the floor must be well documented. The subfloor or gaps between the floor joists and the ground beneath excluding spaces used as cellars and basements must have ventilation that complies with Section 1202.4 of the IBC. The requirement is meant to ensure that there is cross ventilation of the underfloor space. This prevents damp air from turning into water by allowing it to escape. Additionally, it also prevents the accumulation of toxic gases and reduces back-drafting which is dangerous if a fire occurs.

Roof Regulations

All roof assemblies must comply with the requirements of Chapter 15 of the code, and this includes making sure that flashing is installed in a way that does not allow moisture to enter any part of the structure via joints in copings, at meeting points with parapet walls, or through moisture-absorbing materials. Secondary drainage is required if the roof perimeter is built in a way that it rises above the roof surface allowing water to be trapped. Most requirements apply if you add a roof over the original container steel roof.

Joining Regulations

Shipping container homes made of two or more containers stacked or joined together must have no concealed spaces and voids. If a concealed space is present, it must be protected by a fire-resistant joint system that is approved in terms of the regulations. Any new connections particularly in the form of welds must have a strength that matches or exceeds the original weld strength.

Seismic Design Specifications

Regions that experience seismic activities need to think about seismic protection when designing their shipping container home. The requirements are that if a portion or the entire steel wall is intended to resist seismic forces, it should meet the requirements of "light-frame bearing-wall systems with shear panels of all other materials" (ICC, 2020). Most likely, your shipping container home will not be classified as seismic resistant, and an independent system will be required. Independent systems must be designed by structural engineers only. If you are building the container home yourself, you must consult an expert to design the seismic protection system for you.

Simplified Design Requirements

There are designs that are allowed to adopt simplified codes. The guidelines are limited to single unit container homes that meet specific criteria. They are useful to first time DIYers who want to build something simple and get their feet wet with a single unit. The limitations are:

1. The container must be a single unit that exists as a standalone unit and must not be in contact with any other shipping container, building, or structure. If you plan on extending your home by putting a single unit, your build will not meet the criteria that detail simplified design requirements.

2. Rails and corner castings of the container must not be structurally altered, cut, removed, or notched under any circumstances.

3. The container should be installed in the normal orientation, level to the horizontal ground and must be located in an area of seismic category A, B, C, or D. One important regulation for builds meeting the criteria is that the total height must not exceed nine and a half feet.

Legal Requirements in Canada

Shipping container homes in Canada are considered as regular buildings and are regulated in the same manner. The Ontario building code requires buildings larger than 108 sq ft to obtain a building permit before any construction activity. Based on the National Building Code of Canada (NBCC) and the Canadian Standards Association (CSA), the regulations affect both temporary and permanent shipping container structures that are land-based and used for any activity other than transport. Some companies use them as additional storage or on-site space, and their use is regulated by the same codes. Before you start building, you need to notify the local authority. A building inspector must visit where you intend to place the container to check for environmental and safety issues. Some factors considered for approval or disapproval are the stability of the ground, drainage properties, snow loading, risk of the container or delivery truck overturning, structural safety, wind resistance, and anchorage. In Canada, temporary and permanent structures have slightly different requirements, depending on the intended application.

Requirements for Temporary Structures

After an inspection, you must furnish the local council with the detailed site plan, interior layout of the rented container, types of materials to be stored if the structure is used for storage, and the plan and location for man door installation if used as an office. A separate electrical permit is also required by the authorities. In most cases, temporary shipping container structures do not need to obey zoning laws.

Requirements for Permanent Structures

Permanent builds must obey zoning laws which are grouped based on similar structures around the area. It is the owner's responsibility to classify the home as a mobile home, modular building, or manufactured building. This will determine the standard that the structure will be measured against, such as the CSA National Standard for Mobile Home Construction.

Legal Requirements in the UK

The guiding principle is whether the shipping container home translates to material change of use of the land or operational development. It's a grey area in the UK, but in most cases a shipping container home requires a planning permission because while they are classified as temporary structures similar to caravans and mobile homes, they cannot be placed just anywhere. Off limit areas include busy residential areas or areas of outstanding natural beauty.

If you own the land you intend to erect your container structure on, obtaining a planning permit is easy. Before your build, visit the planning portal to determine whether you need a planning permit or not, because some conditions are exempt from a planning permit. For example, if you are extending your home using a shipping container you will not need a permit if the extension does not cover more than half of the land your property is situated on and is not taller than the roof of the original house. Generally, a single container will not take that much space, and a permit will not be needed. Other setups that do not require a planning permit are installing a container home in the garden or converting one into a shed. The size is limited to 65 ft by 22 ft (19.8 m by 6.7 m) dwellings, otherwise a planning permit will be required.

Property Tax

In the UK, shipping container homes may be liable to property tax. If the home is an addition to an existing home that is liable for tax, then you will not be expected to pay additional property tax on your shipping container home. On the other hand, using it as your main house will make you liable for paying property tax to your local council. It can also be considered as a main property if it exceeds the physical footprint limit (not more than half of the land).

Legal Requirements in Australia

In Australia, shipping container homes are regulated similarly to traditional houses. While the requirements vary among states and councils, a permit is required before you can start building a permanent shipping container home. The councils have authority to specify requirements in accordance with Section 254 of the Local Government Act (1999). Structures that are intended to last less than a month on a particular site are considered temporary, and are exempt from this rule. The countryside has similar but relaxed requirements, and permits are needed for homes that are intended to last less than three months.

Some local authorities such as the South Gippsland Council prohibit the use of shipping containers as homes in residential areas. It is important that you check with your local authority if you want to build a shipping container home in Australia because hefty fines can be issued if you breach the regulations. In Barunga West, for example, a planning and building permit is needed for container homes with a footprint larger than 161 sq ft (15 sq m) which represents the floor area almost equivalent to a 20 ft container. Floor space less than this only requires a planning permit by the council. We can't cover the requirements of all the councils here, but the following are generally the factors that are taken into consideration before a home is approved for construction:

Structural Integrity: Plans drawn by a structural engineer or architect are required before you can be allowed to build. The plans must show the structural details and modifications including reinforcements. The foundations must be tied down, regardless of the type of foundation chosen and the tie-down method must be certified by a professional engineer. A means of exiting the container if accidental locking occurs should be detailed. Alternatively, an alarm can be installed to signal distress, and the requirements state that the alarms must be regularly tested for operation.

Zoning: In areas that allow shipping container dwellings to be built, most councils have zones specifying the types of shipping container homes that can be built. Some regions experience regular bushfires and this dictates if you can build a multi-story home or are limited to single units meeting specific fire protections.

Aesthetics: Barunga West Council is one of the district councils that emphasizes aesthetics. Their Shipping Container Home Policy restricts the construction of shipping container homes in zones designated for road reserves and open space areas. All residential areas with space less than half an acre are discouraged from building a container home unless certain conditions are met, such as proof that the structure will not detract from the neighboring properties' amenity.

Building and Subcontracting

DIYers under some jurisdictions such as New South Wales require a builder-owner permit to build their own shipping container homes. The permit allows people with the necessary skills to supervise or build their own home if the value exceeds $10,000 including the labor costs. Other than this, you are limited to keeping the value of your property to under $10,000 which might limit your options. The exception is if development consent is not required. If you go the DIY route and you have the competent skills, then you must be prepared to perform all the tasks specified by the license. These include:

- Supervising work related to the build performed by independent parties
- Ensuring that contractors are appropriately licensed
- Construction site management and purchasing

- Filing and processing of permits
- Ensuring that financial obligations including property tax and property insurance are compliant with state laws, and
- Providing a safe working environment, failure to which can lead to fines and penalties as specified under the Workers Compensation Act 1987 and the Work Health and Safety Act 2011.

Once you have familiarized yourself with the regulations, you can proceed to creating a design with the codes in mind. Try to visit the local authority to get the full list of requirements to ensure that your concept will be compatible with the regulations. It is logical to know what is expected before you put your idea on paper or hire an architect to develop a detailed design.

CHAPTER 3
GETTING STARTED

Your budget will determine the overall detailed design of your project. The money you are willing to invest will determine the sizes of the shipping containers to buy, the quantity and condition, and whether you can go full DIY or hire a contractor. In other words, you need to know what you want to build. Complex builds are more expensive because they will need professional input from architects and structural engineers during the entire building process, starting from the general layout plan. Simple builds are cheaper because less material is required, and little professional help is required. In order to create a detailed design, you must have an idea of your requirements including the intended number of occupants, desired electrical system, and the function of the container home.

Step 1: Determine Your Needs

Your decision on the size of the containers to buy must take your space requirement into consideration. Single-unit shipping container homes make no sense to individuals who are claustrophobic for example. Shipping containers come in different sizes, and standard shipping containers are available in 20 ft (6 m) and 40 ft (12 m) lengths. I've seen 10 ft container cabins, but these are not available as standard purchases. People who build 10 ft shipping container structures usually source from downstream manufacturers who buy and cut regular shipping containers into smaller units. These actually cost more than the standard containers because of the extra labor involved in cutting and joining. You can also find 45 ft containers on the market if you are patient. They are not as common as the 40 ft versions, but the extra five feet is space you should consider investing in if you have the means.

Standard shipping containers are either regular or high cubes which can be either dry cargo or reefers, which are refrigerated. High cube containers are taller. One tip is to consider the taller version if you want comfortable headspace. They offer an additional one foot of vertical space and it's worth it. With this extra space, electrical cabling, air conditioning, and plumbing can be accommodated better without compromising your living space. Of course, a high-cube will be more expensive and usually costs $900 more than a standard container of the same quality and length.

You can also consider a reefer, otherwise known as a refrigerated container if you want to save on insulation costs. Designed to keep contents cold, the insulation is useful to prevent an uncomfortable and noisy home. However, the gain is at the expense of internal space because as much as two feet can be dedicated to the refrigeration equipment and insulation. Apart from this, there is little difference between the external dimensions of general shipping containers that will affect your design. Below are the important dimensions and properties of general purpose shipping containers typically used to construct houses.

- **20 Ft Dry Storage Container**:

  External Measurements

  19 ft 10 in long by 8 ft wide by 8 ft 6 in high

  (6.05 m long by 2.44 m wide by 2.59 m high)

  Internal Measurements

  19 ft 4 in long by 7 ft 8 in wide by 7 ft 10 in high

  (5.9 m long by 2.35 m wide by 2.39 m high)

  The standard weight is 4,960 lbs (2,250 kg) for an empty shipping container with a maximum load capacity of 62,240 lbs (28,230 kg).

- **20 Ft Reefer Container:**

  External Measurements

  Same as the dry storage container.

  Internal Measurements

  17 ft 10 in long by 7 ft 6 in wide by 7 ft 5 in high

  (5.44 m long by 2.28m wide by 2.26m high)

  The standard weight is 6,591 lbs (2,990 kg) empty weight and 67,200 lbs (34,280 kg) maximum load.

- **40 Ft Dry Storage Container:**

  The only difference between this type and a 20 ft container is the length.

  External Length

  40 ft (12.19 m)

  Internal Length

  39 ft 6 in (12.04 m)

  The standard weight is 8,333 lbs (3,780 kg) empty weight with a maximum loading capacity of 58,863 lbs (27,600 kg).

- **40 Ft Reefer Container:**

  External Measurements

  Same as the dry storage container.

  Internal Measurements

  37.9 ft by 7.5 ft wide by 7.4 ft high

  (11.58 m long by 2.28 m wide by 2.25 m high)

  The standard weight is 9,965 lbs (4,520 kg) empty weight with a maximum loading capacity of 74,957 lbs (34,000 kg).

All high cube containers have an additional one foot vertical space. There are slight variations because of the acceptable tolerances from the ISO standards that manufacturers follow, and you might find the empty weight and dimensions displayed on the container's identifying plate to be different from the standards. Manufacturers tend to go beyond the minimum weight specifications enforced by ISO standards to make their products more robust. The ISO specifications can serve as a guide for your design, but you will need to match the actual dimensions of the container with your design by checking with the manufacturer. If you choose a reefer, take note of the patch work that will follow the removal of the refrigeration components. It also has a different floor structure, made of aluminum T-sections. Reefers are usually more expensive as well, at times costing one and a half times more than a standard container.

Step 2: Create a Design

After choosing the preferred container specifications to suit your requirements, it will be easy to sketch some designs without the need of a designer or architect. Better yet, you can use some free software to help you with the floor plans and layout if you are tech savvy. Personally I use SketchUp Make because it offers me a lot of possibilities, including the ability to import components designed by other people. Other capable software include Live Home 3D and 3D ISBU Shipping Container Home and Floorplanner. Pick one that you are comfortable using.

You can decide to have multifunctional rooms that can help you take advantage of the space. Other options include complementing the shipping container home with extensions made from wood, or using the original doors as walls to create additional space. Important factors you also need to consider include humidity, climate, and potential hazards. Knowing this will help you have an idea about the type of foundation you need as well as the anchoring, and whether or not you require insulation. When creating a design, consider the eco-friendliness rating that you want to achieve.

After you have put your idea on paper, take your concept to a structural engineer so that they can specify the type of foundations for the plans to be submitted to the local authority. Structural engineers are also responsible for detailing the required structural reinforcements. This step will make sure that you stay within budget without having to worry about your build not holding up or complying with building codes. Make sure that you are advised on the scope of work, because this step will also help you choose either the DIY or subcontracting route.

Eco-Friendliness Rating

Re-using a shipping container on its own does not translate into eco-friendliness. The rating your house will achieve depends on your location and the assessing party. In general, certifications in each country are managed by the Green Building Councils. The councils provide the criteria needed to achieve specific tiers of eco-friendliness, and the higher the score, the more sustainable your home is considered. The differences in each county lie on the evaluation system used and the resulting classification, but usually there are four tiers awarded, namely certified (40 - 49 points), silver (50 - 59 points), gold (60 - 79 points) and platinum (over 80 points).

LEED is one of the popular green building evaluation systems that has been adopted by a number of countries worldwide. It is classified as a third-party rating system, and certification is based on a 100-point scale. When rating a home using the LEED system, nine components are considered. The main criteria are the sustainability of the location, the building materials and resources used, indoor conditions, and water efficiency. The objectives of the next generation model of LEED green building standards are focused on reducing greenhouse gas emissions and promoting human health during construction and occupation of homes. This update includes the evaluation of shipping container homes. Certification is only possible after the container home has been permanently installed on-site, but you can review the requirements to get an idea of eco-friendly elements you should incorporate into your design.

Step 3: Submit the Paperwork

Once you are satisfied with your idea and have created a detailed set of plans, submit your plans for approval. Expect to pay application fees to process the application and be prepared for a little back and forth with the building officer. They usually require further details, especially if you are dealing with a local authority that has little experience with shipping container homes. While your papers are being processed, you can go ahead with purchasing your containers if you are confident that you meet the requirements of the local authority. Other activities related to preparing for the physical work can also be done according to the timeline of your project schedule.

Step 4: Buy the Container

Buying a shipping container is a straightforward process. You have the luxury of choosing containers based on their condition, and your budget will determine whether you will buy a new container, a one-trip container, or a used container. One-trip shipping containers will have been used once and are usually in pristine condition. Many of them are practically new, and there is little difference in terms of durability between them and a new container.

Pros of a New Shipping Container

The major advantage with a new container is that you will be certain that nothing toxic has been inside. This will make your cleaning work before the build less involved. If sourcing locally, there is some guarantee that it has not been exposed to marine conditions and stress that may compromise its structural integrity. If you live in a cold climate, buying a new shipping container offers you the possibility of having the hardwood floor excluded, and installing a new floor that meets the floor insulation standards will be easier compared to stripping the floor from a used container.

You can also ask the manufacturer to not treat the hardwood floor using pesticides, since the container will not be used to carry cargo. Keruing and Apitong are the common types of wood used to make the floors because of their resilience against harsh conditions. The problem is that they also attract pests and this is why manufacturers are required by law to treat the floors with pesticide.

Buying a brand new shipping container means that you will not need to fix any damages, such as rust and dents. The containers will be ready to convert immediately after delivery. You will also be able to obtain the technical specifications of the container such as the distance between the centers of the corner casts, which will allow you to prepare for the building work without having to physically inspect the containers. Purchasing a new container is also a smart idea if you want to reduce the work during your build, because you can order your container with custom-cut profiles. This way, there is some certainty that the end-result is a structurally sound product. If you decide to have the openings cut at the factory, expect to pay more to the purchase price, because of the additional labor costs. The manufacturer will cut to your specifications, so be sure to provide accurate measurements.

Most shipping containers are produced in China and exported to the global market. Only a small fraction of containers are manufactured in the United States, the UK, and Australia. If you are based in the United States and want to buy a shipping container directly from the manufacturer, W&K Container Inc. manufactures containers in the United States. Shipping container home builders in the UK can source from YMC Container Solutions. In Canada, ATS containers is one of the leading suppliers of new containers and Australians can buy new shipping containers from SCF.

Alternatively, a one-trip container can be purchased. Since the container will have been used to carry cargo once after it has been purchased from the manufacturer, most DIYers prefer using them over a new container. They are usually less than one year old and are not classified as used containers. One trip containers are the next best thing to a new container for markets that do not have a local manufacturer.

Cons of a New Shipping Container

When new containers are manufactured, new carbon dioxide is released into the environment. There is no sustainability in using a new shipping container to build a home, and doing so does not solve the climate problem. The idea is to recycle old containers and reduce the carbon footprint that is attached with abandoned containers.

There is also no financial incentive to build a home using new containers. One of the reasons I build container homes is that they offer quality homes at a lower price point. It is not unusual to find a new shipping container costing three times more than a good quality used shipping container.

Used Shipping Container

Used shipping containers are affordable and justify the alternative home argument. By repurposing an old shipping container, recyclers save money on melting, and the builder saves on housing costs. In the United States, a used shipping container can cost between $3,000 and $5,000, while new and one-trip shipping containers will set you back between $5,000 and $9,000. In the UK, the average price of a used container is £1,500 if you source from popular sites like eBay and Gumtree. In Australia and Canada, a used shipping container can cost between $3,000 and $5,000 in local currency.

On the other hand, used containers are on average at least eight years old before shipping companies consider letting them go. Sometimes they will have dents, scratches, and rust because of the wear and tear during their lifecycle. If the container is badly damaged, the amount of work involved can be discouraging for a beginner. You will have to be committed to cutting out the wall sections yourself or hire somebody with the necessary equipment to do it.

Some containers may not have identification plates. When I started building shipping container houses, I utilized containers that had been abandoned. They had no tags which made it difficult to determine the types of pesticides used. In the end, the hardwood floors had to be stripped and a new floor installed. Fortunately, there were no regulations in existence at the time, so this did not have an implication on the building permits. If you want to save, scout for abandoned containers at the shipyards, ports, and in areas where the logistics industry is vibrant. Chances are you will find containers that still have the identification plates attached. If you cannot find abandoned containers and you are on a budget, consider buying used containers instead. In the industry, a used container means it is no longer useful to a transport company.

The cost to buy a used shipping container depends on the size, type and condition. Smaller containers are slightly cheaper than larger containers of the same size per unit. However, if you consider the price per unit area, the larger containers are cheaper because the price difference is usually less than $1,000. Smaller containers are more expensive per unit because they are in greater demand. They are easier to handle and cheaper to transport, and will therefore cost less to operate for shipping companies. Nowadays you can easily find a used shipping container to buy online. There are tons of classifieds that you can visit, similar to how you buy a car or furniture. Some builders have managed to buy used containers from Craigslist for as little as $1,000.

Buying Tips

Here are a few things to consider when buying a used shipping container to convert into a home.

Selecting: Choose the container type and check for the specifications on the identification plate also known as the CSC plate. Although you might not use it, the CSC number will help you verify ownership and container specifications. Make an attempt to buy locally, to reduce delivery costs. If the paperwork is missing, buying locally can also help you go back to the seller to get the necessary information that might be needed for building permits, and it makes the inspection part convenient. Some local authorities require the identification plate to be visible during the initial inspections, so remember to check this requirement.

Inspecting: Conduct an inspection or ask for an inspection report. Your inspection will help you assess the condition of the container and determine if repairs are required. Check the roof, bottom parts, and the door locks for rust and deformations. If the frame of the container does not look straight, do not buy the container. You will have problems leveling the container itself and anything else you might want to install.

Sometimes used containers will have patches that are welded, indicating that they have been repaired. The lining of the door must be intact, otherwise you will not get a watertight seal if it rains. The latches that the door locks into should be in good condition and you should test the locking mechanism to determine if it moves freely. The doors are heavy, so checking them makes sure that they open and close properly. The roof must also be checked. If you see bulging and sagging, beam supports will be needed to restore the roof to its original shape. You will not be able to panel beat it into shape, so consider this before buying the container. If you are a beginner, it's best to avoid containers with roofs that are out of shape.

In addition to this, you might have to consider a smell test if you are concerned about any toxic residue that could affect your health. If you cannot inspect in person, always consider requesting an inspection report and images of the product. The images must include all the details that we have mentioned above. Written inspection reports are important because they provide you with an assurance of the container's structural integrity and an idea of the contents that have been in the container. Some local authorities also require it to issue the building permits. Ensure that the smell test is included in the report.

Verification: Identify the manufacturer of the shipping container. This is important if you plan on using multiple containers to complete your build. Remember that although the ISO standards guide manufacturers, there are variations in the dimensions according to the manufacturer. Ask the seller to accurately measure the distance between the four bottom corners so that you can prepare for the foundation before the container arrives. If you will be using multiple containers, it is also advisable to buy containers made by the same manufacturer for uniformity. Discuss delivery options with the seller.

Transporting the Container

Not all sellers provide transport as part of your purchase, and you may need to arrange transport yourself. Companies offering transport consider the weight of the container, its dimensions, and the availability of drivers and the distance. With the fluctuations in gas prices, the cost to transport is calculated on a case-by-case basis. Once the specifications have been determined, a transport company can provide a quote along with the necessary paperwork and route planning to ensure that your container is delivered to the construction site.

If your construction site is less than 200 miles (321 km) from the origin, a tilt bed truck is the most cost effective choice of transport. Tilt bed trucks have a bed that can slide a container into place by tilting the bed at an angle, letting gravity do the work. No additional equipment is necessary to position the container onto the foundation. Even if the container is empty, the site must have dry and firm ground that is level to ensure that the truck can successfully deliver the payload. You also need to ensure that there is enough space for the truck to maneuver because a lot of driving back and forth is required to precisely position the container. Trees, powerlines, and water bodies are examples of barriers that can disturb the process.

Sites that are located more than 200 miles away require a flatbed truck to deliver a shipping container home. While they are cost effective in delivering shipping containers over long distances, the downside is that additional equipment is required. You may need to hire a crane or forklift to move the container from the truck and place it on the foundation. Cranes are preferred, because they can be rigged at the corner casts to make the placement safe and easy. If you decide to operate the crane yourself, you must check if you need special licences to operate the equipment. When using a forklift, it is important to note that if the equipment is not used correctly the floor of the container can be damaged. 20 ft containers should be moved using forklifts fitted with 6 ft long tines. 40 ft containers, on the other hand, need 8 ft long tines, otherwise you risk damaging the floor. Ordinary warehouse forklifts must not be used to move shipping containers, and when leasing the equipment it is important to ensure that the forklift is rated for loads that are 15,000 lbs (6,804 kg) and over. It is a simple pick and drop since shipping containers are fitted with forklift pockets.

If you decide on a high cube container, you will need to transport it with a step-deck truck because these trucks are lower to the ground. They are designed to compensate for the extra one foot of the container's height, and like the flat bed truck, additional equipment is needed. It is important that you follow the instructions provided, so that you do not risk the container slipping off a forklift, or falling from improperly secured rigging. Hiring the equipment and the operator is recommended.

Some regions have an extensive rail network. This can be a viable option, although it is location specific. I have never considered this option for my builds because the requirements and paperwork is demanding, and this can make it costly. Part of the reason is that trains usually carry shipping containers with loaded cargo, and usually a cargo manifest is required. In most cases, it is cheaper and more convenient to transport your shipping container by road.

Moving the Container on Your Property

Often, people will want to move their shipping container home within their own premises. Sometimes they don't like the location or prefer to complete the build before placing it on the foundation. Instead of going back to the Stone Age and jacking your container to put rollers on, consider buying wheel sets. There are over a dozen designs of wheel that can be attached to the corner castings to facilitate moving the container via towing. The Australian market in particular has some unique wheels that are identical to car tires. These are one of the best sets to use to move a shipping container over short distances if you are pulling using a truck or tractor. Other markets also have wheels such as castor wheels, and you may have to choose your wheel attachments based on the equipment you have access to. This solution only works for single container homes. Multi-story and conjoined shipping container homes are impossible to move using this method. You will need to hire capable equipment to do that.

CHAPTER 4
TOOLS AND EQUIPMENT

DIY container home builds require tools to help you do the job. This is hardly a one-person job, so be sure to organize all the help you need. For a simple construction, two people can successfully complete the project. You will need to subcontract some parts of the build, depending on the choice of foundation, insulation material, and size of the project. The basic tools that you will need include cutting tools, drills, and measuring devices, not forgetting your safety gear. I have included a list of specialty tools you may need to purchase or rent for your build.

Excavation Equipment

Your requirements will be greatly influenced by the topography of your site and the foundation you plan on building. Rough, hilly terrain with obstacles such as big rocks will require you to excavate the land using earthmoving machinery. This equipment will need to be rented by the hour, and the costs can be staggering if you want to clear a large portion. Visit a local company to assess the cost of leasing equipment or you can try to borrow some equipment from your neighbors if available. Some companies offer both wet and dry leasing options if you have the license to operate the machinery. If you intend on building a full concrete slab foundation, an excavator and compactor may be required as well. Their purpose is to create a flatbed for the concrete to rest on.

Simple foundations, like a pier foundation, and relatively flat and firm ground can make use of hand tools. A regular wheelbarrow and shovel can get the job done. You can also get away with a hand compactor to make sure that the soil is packed tightly before pouring the concrete.

Foundation Building Equipment

Full concrete foundations consume a decent amount of concrete. For this type of foundation, it is cost effective and ultimately saves you on labor if you order concrete delivered by mixing trucks. Some concrete delivery trucks are equipped with vibrators for driving out the air to reduce air pockets. If you need a lot of concrete, you will need to allocate enough time between the loads and driving air bubbles out. If the foundation is a pier foundation, a mixing bucket and a power drill with a mixing tool will be sufficient. After all, you will be mixing small batches of concrete, which will be placed in a mold. Shovels and a wheelbarrow are also required for this step.

Cutting Tools

Without openings, a shipping container is just a metal box. The container's corrugated walls are 14 gauge thick (0.075 inches) therefore you will need either an angle grinder, plasma cutter, or a cutting torch. The depth of the corrugation is one inch either side and two inches at the back. The corrugation depths are the reason the interior and exterior dimensions differ. The frame is thicker, measuring at two inches so you will need capable tools. There are a few options on the market to suit every budget and skill.

Angle Grinder: This is your cheapest option, and angle grinders are easy to use. Since you will be cutting heavy metal, investing in diamond coated cutting and grinding discs will save you some money in the long run. It is not uncommon for a DIYer to consume as much as 100 general purpose cutting discs on a single project. Diamond cutting discs are harder and last longer than ordinary cutting discs. In addition, you might need a reciprocating saw if your design requires you to make small and precise cuts. The circular profile of an angle grider's cutting disc can make it difficult to make precise non-rectangular cuts that you may need to make for bespoke designs.

Plasma Cutter: Plasma cutting offers you cleaner cuts, and the equipment is less physically demanding to operate than angle grinders, because the operation of angle grinders results in gyroscopic forces being generated. This is the vibration you feel when cutting through thick metal. The downside is that the price of plasma cutters is not worth it if you intend to build a single shipping container home. Only buy it if you plan on completing big projects.

Cutting Torch: You can opt for an oxyacetylene torch cutter if you want an affordable and fast way to cut. They are a bit tricky to operate because they need to be properly set up. You will also need to buy the gas tanks for oxygen and acetylene that are used during the cutting process. If you don't have the skills to set up the equipment, you're better off choosing an angle grinder because improper setup will result in cutting slag that will need to be ground off, creating more work for you. In any case, you will need an angle grinder to smoothen out any rough edges that result from the cutting process.

Other important tools that you will need to complete the job include power drills, screwdrivers, and measuring devices to use when installing fixtures. This list provided above is not exhaustive, so later on in the book when we discuss some conversion projects, a comprehensive list of tools and materials required will be included for each project.

Welding Equipment

While you can get away with a no-weld shipping container home, welding is the optimal choice when building a shipping container home. If you are going to weld, the build needs to be robust and good-looking to pass the building officer's scrutiny. Remember the IBC G151-18 code requires welds to be of strength equal to or greater than the original weld. If you do not have the welding skills, you must hire a professional welder. They charge by the hour or per job depending on your location. Always ask for certification to make sure that the outcome is of acceptable standard. Welding is required for connecting the container to the foundation, joining containers together, and fixing the doors and windows to the body as well as any structural supports. DIYers can choose the Gas Arc Metal Welder (MIG welder), Shielded Metal Arc Welder (stick welder), Tungsten Arc Welder (TIG welder) as all of them are suitable options.

Stick welders are suitable for thick welds, but they are difficult for a beginner to use and are labor intensive. Take some practice lessons to learn how to use a stick welder. MIG welders on the other hand are easy to use, but they are not suitable for thick welds. You will need an expensive version of MIG welder if you want to weld thick sections together. If your skills are lacking, you might want to outsource the job or avoid designs that require thick welds altogether. You also need to consider the electricity supply you have access to. In the US and Canada, the standard power supply is 110V/120V, and a MIG welder of this rating can only weld sections up to 3/16 inches (0.46725 cm) thick. The UK and Australia have 220V as standard, and a suitably rated MIG welder can weld thicker sections. You can expect to pay around $900 for a dual (110V/220V) MIG welder if you have access to a 220V power supply.

Insulation Spraying Gear

Open-cell and closed-cell insulation require specialized equipment to apply. Your choice of equipment depends on the size of the area that needs to be insulated. We will get to insulation options later in the book, but if you have to insulate your home yourself using spray foam, a spray gun kit with cartridges (cylinders) is your best bet. This option is cost effective if you need to insulate a small house, and off the grid, otherwise the cost of the cylinders might exceed hiring a professional. The other options are industrial grade insulation machines, and these are expensive to purchase. Only consider this equipment for commercial purposes.

Other options include homemade spray foam insulation kits. You will need to purchase the plans to make the kit. The two major components are an air compressor and a spray gun for applying spray foam insulation. This is an option if you have to insulate a big area, or plan on converting a number of shipping containers in the future. Spray guns are rated based on the pressure, volume, and spray velocity required, and you will need to match their specifications with the compressor you own or intend to purchase. Remember to purchase the protective equipment necessary to avoid breathing in spray foam particles and to protect your skin. The spray foam can irritate the skin if there is contact.

Carpentry Tools

The frames are more economical if a wooden frame is used. You will need tools such as a circular saw and jigsaw to cut the wood. Hand tools can also be used, but using them is time consuming, and the final structure may not look neat compared to a frame that has members cut using power tools. Joining the wooden pieces will also require a nail gun and braces or clamps to hold the parts in position. If you are not in the DIY community, it is advisable to visit the local hardware store to check out the options available to you.

Finishing Tools

Chances are you may want to paint the interior and exterior walls of your completed home. For a quality finish, a spray gun powered by a compressor is the best equipment to use. It is important to match the spray gun to the compressor, otherwise you may end up with a gun that splatters paint all over if the compressor you are using is small. Look for a compressor that can achieve at least eight bars of pressure. This pressure must also be matched with the specified volume of air that the spray gun requires.

CHAPTER 5
BUILDING PROCEDURES

Once everything is in place, the real work starts. To avoid delays, ensure that you have the correct tools before starting. One tip is to run the build in your mind to help you visualize the process. This will help you allocate resources sequentially, especially if you are not keen on buying the entire tool shop, or intend to subcontract some parts of the build. When I visualize my build, I write down the steps and jot down the resources required for each step to determine what to DIY and what to outsource.

Step 5: Prepare the Site

Site preparation is required for obvious reasons. Besides clearing the area to ensure that the delivery truck will have room to move around, preparing the site will also protect the container and surroundings from damage. You should check the potential site for any installations such as power lines, septic tanks, water spigots, and other buildings. Choose a site that is flat, compact and firm, because on soft ground, the shifting weight distribution can cause uneven sinking. The site should be checked for sloping so that runoff water is properly directed away from the property. If you are connecting to the grid, then you should also consider access to utilities when deciding where to place your container home. This should be followed by compacting and leveling the land. You will need to rent or borrow an excavator and a compactor to ensure that your installation will be flat, and in some cases you can also use this equipment to dig the trenches you will need for your foundation.

Choosing a Location

Consider how nature interacts with your proposed site. The way the sun interacts with your container home will affect some aspects of your life. The sun's position relative to your house throughout the day is important. Solar installations must be exposed to the sun as much as possible during the day. Make sure that the house will be oriented in a way that will provide the necessary exposure to the sun. I made this mistake and built a roof without considering the position of the sun in the sky. In the end, the panels only received three hours of direct exposure to the sun. Eventually, the panels had to be relocated to a new structure independent of the container home so that the energy needs could be met.

Another reason to consider the home's position relative to the sun is that the rising sun can add warmth and natural light inside your home. This is a good thing in cold climates, but if you are located in a hot climate, the internal temperatures can rise quickly, requiring you to run your air conditioning unit longer to keep you comfortable during the day.

Checking the drainage is also important because during the rainy season, you do not want to stay in a flooded home. Insects like mosquitoes also breed in still water, putting you at risk of contracting diseases.

Off-grid builds that include a concrete foundation need to have a water source close. The water is useful when curing the concrete regardless of whether the concrete is delivered pre-mixed or prepared on-site. If there is no running water on site, the water can be delivered by a truck and stored in a water tank. Before choosing an off-grid site, it is a good idea to have the water table determined. This step will help you decide if you must have a borehole drilled or a shallow well dug for you to have water supply.

Marking Out Areas

Once you are satisfied with the results of your survey, you should mark out the corners to indicate where the container home will be built. If you are connecting to the grid, identify the route for the pipe that connects to the sewer system. The pipe to the sewage must not be too long. If the pipe is long, you may have trouble getting the waste to properly flow into the sewer system. Each state publishes the maximum recommended length of the sewer pipe. You can find this information in the building codes.

Stake out the marked areas and begin excavating the water lines and sewer lines towards the foundation area. It's important to start with this so that there is alignment between the outlets and the main lines. You must avoid complex connections to the main utility lines as much as possible. Direct connections without bends are recommended because if your pipes have too many bends, your system can experience higher frictional losses which will make the water flow slower than required for the system to function properly.

Step 6: Lay the Foundation

Without a foundation, your container home will not have a base to support its weight and the contents of your home. It is rare to find ground that is materially uniform. Often, the soil is mixed with stones to some extent. The natural shifting of the ground from loading will leave your house uneven over time. This can result in doors that are difficult to open for example, and in worst case scenarios, place structural stress on your structure. Build your foundation before the container arrives. If the container is delivered before the foundation is ready, you will have to rent additional equipment to position the container again when the foundation is ready, and the costs can go out of hand, especially if you are connecting the containers together vertically using rented equipment.

First you will need to choose what type of foundation you want to put your home on, but fortunately, you are spoilt for choice when it comes to the types of foundation to install. Your options depend on the geology, budget, and number of containers used in the build. All foundations must be dug to depths below the frost line. This varies from state to state, and you can check the requirements in your area by referring to the National Snow and Ice Data Center.

Types of Foundations for Container Homes

Wood Beams: If you are on a budget, wood beams are cost effective solutions that can be versatile. Usually, they are posts that are placed at each corner of the container for as many containers you have and buried partially underground. The disadvantage is that they work best for temporary installations and might not be an ideal choice if your home is to stay for an extended period in a particular location. Another downside is that wood is susceptible to rot. You will need to treat the wood properly and take preventative measures to ensure that the wood is not exposed to moisture, otherwise your foundation will weaken over time. Choose engineered wood that is rated to support heavy loads if you prefer to build a wooden foundation. Parts that will be buried in the ground may be treated with bitumen and termite poison.

Full Concrete Slab: Permanent builds can use a foundation of poured concrete. It is easier to have the concrete delivered by a mixer truck, so the concrete will be of superior quality, and pouring it will be an easy task. Generally you need the assistance of a professional if you decide on a full concrete slab. It is also an expensive process, because you will need to pour concrete to cover the entire floor area plus the overlap. Often, the delivery truck only supplies the product. This means that you have to get a contractor to help you place reinforcement steel if this has been specified by the structural engineer. On stable ground, the reinforcement may not be necessary because a full concrete slab foundation evenly distributes the weight of the shipping containers over its surface area.

Pier Foundation: Pier foundations are a popular choice with DIYers, because they are cheap, and they are simple to construct since piers are basically concrete blocks. Typically they measure half a meter for each dimension, and they are positioned on each corner for a 20ft container. The longer shipping containers will need extra piers midway to fully support the shipping container throughout its length. When I was helping an elderly couple build their tiny shipping container home, the piers they made themselves easily passed the inspection of the building officer. If an elderly couple can do it DIY, there is no reason why other people cannot. Little technical input required. One thing to note is that this type of foundation must be reinforced with rebar. The container's weight places a concentrated load on each pillar, and the rebar helps to increase the compressive and tensile strength of the concrete. Although the house will rarely experience tensile forces, natural events such as hurricanes and earthquakes can generate shear stress forces on the structure, causing lateral forces which can lead to possible failure where the container and the piers are connected. This is why it is recommended to weld a steel plate to anchor the container to the foundation. Other than this, choosing a pier foundation is the best choice for your DIY build.

Strip Foundation: This foundation is also known as a trench foundation. The strips are usually between one and two feet in diameter and set four feet deep and filled with concrete. They resemble a combination between a full concrete slab and a pier foundation, making them a cheaper alternative to a full concrete slab. The downside is that they have a low resistance to earthquakes and tremors, so if your area has frequent earthquakes, stay away from strip foundations. Reinforcements can help, but you will require a considerable amount of steel for the foundation to withstand seismic forces. Only use the foundation for small and medium builds, and in regions that do not experience earthquakes.

Pile Foundation: This type of foundation is expensive, because it requires a professional with pile driving equipment to install. The foundation consists of cylindrical and solid steel tubes that are driven into the ground until suitable load bearing capacity is reached. If the ground you want to build your home on has weak soil, you must use piles to support the container home. Since they go deep into the ground until the structural engineer has determined that the desired ground stability has been reached, the costs to install vary significantly. After pile driving, the foundation is capped with concrete blocks and after installation, they will resemble a pier foundation.

Ventilating the Foundation

The space underneath non-slab foundations is known as crawl space and if there is no air circulation, the wooden floor can develop rot and mold as a result of condensation. According to the regulations, foundation types that create crawl spaces must be ventilated in order to prevent moisture from building up underneath the container as a result of condensation. This means strip and pier foundations will require ventilation. Strip and pier foundations can be ventilated using two methods, venting and dehumidifying. There is no need to cut the floor of the container. You can ventilate the crawl space by using air vents that are fitted with a wire mesh to prevent snakes and insects from getting inside the foundation. You must pay attention to the climate before venting the foundation. In cold climates, venting the subfloor is effective and you may not need to insulate the floor. Venting the foundation in humid climates can be problematic because the outside air contains moisture that will condense inside the crawl space. The remedy is to install a dehumidifier in the crawl space or seal the space to prevent humid air from getting in.

Step 7: Place, Clean, Cut, and Join

After your foundation is set and approved, the next step is to place the shipping containers in position. Since this is usually done on delivery depending on the mode of transport, it should be an easy task. Once positioned, get down to business and start cleaning your container. First, inspect the inside and outside to check if there is anything you missed from your pre-purchase inspection to determine the cleaning products you need and if you need to purchase rust remover. When purchasing cleaning chemicals, the only rule is to pick detergent suitable for use on steel. Sweep the container floor thoroughly, and note the condition of the floor and the type of material used. The pesticide used to prevent parasites from damaging the floor is usually not harmful to humans on contact, and some people prefer to keep the original flooring. Sometimes, however, the pesticides can be toxic, so each manufacturer lists the pesticide they apply. You can find information on the type of pesticide used on the container's identification plate. If you are concerned about the pesticides used, you may have to remove the entire floor.

Be sure to avoid sanding the original wood in an attempt to clean the wooden surface if you are keeping it and plan to put varnish over it. The pesticide treatment goes deeper beneath the surface and you will generate toxic fumes by sanding. Later on I will provide you with options you can choose for your floor that will prevent you from inhaling toxic fumes when working with the original floor

Cutting the Openings

Part of the IBC's rules require single unit containers to have openings that are less than half the size of the corrugated walls. I have seen designs that involve cutting the entire wall out and replacing it with a framed glass sliding door. Check with the codes to see if this is allowed. Before you start cutting, grab some painter's tape or a marker and mark out the cutouts so that you can have more precise cuts. The measure twice, cut once rule must be followed, so that you avoid cutting parts that you don't need removed. Mistakes made will have to be corrected. It may be difficult to do this if you don't have the right skills. Remember to avoid cutting any part of the frame, especially the corner casings. This will weaken the structure, and your house may not pass the inspection.

When cutting the window and door openings, start with the smallest sections. For first time DIYers especially, cutting may seem like a simple process, but the resistance of the material makes it difficult if you are using a 710 W angle grinder. Starting with small cuts will help you get the feel of the process and will prevent injury if a heavy metal section falls accidentally. Choose thin cutting discs to make your cuts faster and less labor intensive. Thin cutting discs will feel like a hot knife through butter compared to thick discs.

Remember to have your safety boots, gloves and glasses when you cut the walls. I always advise my clients to break down large openings into small sections to make it easier to manage. You must also cut the openings for the electrical cabling, ventilation, plumbing and waste water drainage. In the IBC code, these openings have specific requirements that will be demonstrated in the example builds.

Rust Treatment

If your containers are beat up and rusty, they must be treated before joining to ensure a strong bond. Invest in a wire brush and sandpaper or a sander to clean the rust off until fresh bare metal is exposed. If you notice that sections of the remaining wall have been badly corroded by rust, you can patch over the holes with the window and door pieces you've already cut out. The patches will need to be welded to the walls of the container from the outside. Make sure the welds run through the entire seam to avoid water leaking into the insulation. Grab a can of ceramic paint or elastic paint to seal the patches. This is important especially if your welding skills are poor. It is difficult for a beginner welder to have a continuous weld bead, and sometimes there will be tiny holes embedded in the weld bead. These holes can trap moisture, causing the joint to develop more rust and weaken.

Joining

If you plan on building a temporary structure, bolts and clamps provide stable connections that are easy to remove. You will save time when disassembling your build to move it to a different location. Unlike welding, bolts do not provide an equally strong connection, although they are cheap. You can make use of the corner castings and use them as connection points for your containers. There are various clamps on the market designed for connecting containers together, although they are expensive. In the UK, Container Clamps manufactures robust clamps and these can be purchased online from different vendors across many countries. You can also check out other manufacturers—just be sure to check the quality and specifications of the product.

The favorite joining method when building a shipping container home is welding. Welding is a permanent way to connect several shipping containers together, and is a skill that gets better with time. It took me three months of practice to start producing quality welds when I started building shipping container homes. The major problem I encountered was burning through the metal because of staying too long on one spot. Before you start welding, practice on a few scrap pieces to assess the quality of your weld. Controlling the temperature is important when you are joining the openings' frames to the container walls. Choose equipment that is forgiving of beginner mistakes if you want to carry out the welds yourself.

My choice of welding equipment is a stick welder. I find it easier to use, although this is a subjective assessment. If you choose a stick welder, choose the welding rods carefully. They come in different sizes which gives them different bonding properties. To choose the correct welding rods, consider the following:

Base Metal Properties: You will be welding steel sections together. Choose an electrode that is designed to weld two different types of steel together, because it is likely that you will not find corten steel to use for framing and structural support. I find the E7018 welding rod the best electrode to use when joining the two materials. It will produce a weld that has the same weathering properties of the corten steel used to make shipping containers. It is recommended for use if you intend to complete the weld in one pass and on materials that are less than 10 mm in thickness. You will not need rods meant for thicker material, because the thickest part of a shipping container is the bottom frame which is 0.017 in (4.5 mm) thick.

Tensile Strength: Welding rods are marked to indicate the tensile strength of the resulting weld. The tensile strength of the welding rod must match or exceed the tensile strength of the materials to be joined. The E7018 welding rod is rated at 82,670 psi and works well for corten steel which has a tensile strength of 80,000 psi.

Other advantages of the e7018 welding electrodes are their ability to form strong bonds in most environments, and that it can be used to weld in horizontal, vertical, flat, and overhead positions. This is important because you may need to weld the shipping container from several positions as you complete the build.

Welding Procedure

Industrial welding requires welding procedures to be used for welding structural elements. For a DIY build, a welding procedure is an overkill because of the amount of technical information and qualifications required. However, there is no harm in borrowing some concepts of welding procedures to make sure that DIY welds are structurally sound. The surfaces to be joined must be clean and dry. Apart from this, there are five essentials to ensuring a good weld. You need to choose the correct electrode size and set the correct current, voltage, and travel speed. You will also need to position your electrode at the correct angle.

Electrode Size: To choose the correct electrode diameter, you must consider the position of the area to be welded, the gap between the material to be joined, and the electrode's ability to allow current flow without reducing its deposition properties. When welding two metals, heat stresses are set up, and this can cause the metals to distort. The rule is to choose rods that generate low heat when welding thin sections. This is useful if you are welding the window frames to the corrugated wall sections.

Welding Current: Select the optimum current for the materials you intend to join. If the current is too low, the heat generated is not sufficient to melt the base metal. On the other hand, a high current will consume your electrodes too quickly, resulting in an irregular weld.

Welding Voltage or Arc Length: High voltage melts the electrode in large quantities resulting in poor fusion between the metals to be joined and the filler material. Low voltages cause the electrode to stick to the material being joined because the electrode will not melt. Again, this causes poor fusion between the materials to be joined, resulting in a weak weld.

Weld Speed: Your ability to weld is determined by how well you can control the speed to the electrode. It takes practice to know how fast the electrode must travel over the materials to be joined. If you move the electrode too fast, the weld pool will not last. This causes impurities and gasses to be trapped inside the weld, leading to a weak joint. Moving the electrode too slowly will cause the filler metal to pile up, resulting in a wide deposit that will need to be ground off.

Welding Angle: If you plan on doing multi-pass welds, you must hold the electrode at an angle that will allow the weld to have a good bead shape. This is very important for aesthetics in fillet and deep groove welding. These are welds that have the weld filling in between the materials to be joined. Two things affect the weld angle. The work angle is one of the components, and it is determined by the surrounding conditions. You must work in a comfortable position to have a good work angle. On the other hand, the travel angle is the angle along the direction of the weld. Usually it varies between 5 and 30 degrees.

CHAPTER 6
REINFORCING THE STRUCTURE

Multi-container builds that are connected together have to be supported at the joints, where the frames meet. These resemble pillars, although you can weld horizontal supports above the roof to prevent the roof sections from collapsing where the frames of different containers meet. Welding horizontal cross bars is recommended if the roof is designed to carry loads above it. Rooftop decks and patios will need you to install cross beams over or under the roof. If you are installing air conditioners, it is better to weld the supports for the units before insulating or building the wall so that there is no additional cutting. The openings must be framed so that it is easy to replace units that become faulty. The walls also need to be held in place, and this is usually achieved by framing the interior.

Step 8: Weld the Supports

If you cut the entire wall out when joining several containers to create more space, you need to support the frame vertically with metal posts. Two vertical beams are sufficient to support the roof when two 40 ft containers are butt joined together. The rule of thumb is that you need as many beams as the number of containers you are using. The roof of the container is very heavy, so reinforcements are necessary if you want the house to pass inspections. They must be welded, because bolting them in place does not provide adequate strength to maintain the original connection strength. Besides, drilling holes through the frame will not be easy using a hand drill because of the thickness of the metal. Cut-outs for window and door sections must be framed to allow you to install the windows. The IBC code is specific to this requirement and usually the material of choice is a steel square tube profile. You can also use angle iron if you want to save money. The only difference is that it will affect the type of window frames that you will install and the wooden frame where your electrical wiring, plumbing, and insulation will go. It is good practice to have an interior that is smooth and free of protruding elements.

Step 9: Installing Windows and Doors

I recommend installing the windows and doors before building the frame or installing the walls. That way, if you have made the mistake of cutting large holes, you can fix the problem by compensating with the wall material by leaving an overlap. Covering with trim will hide your beginner's mistakes. Another reason to install the windows and doors first is that if you install the insulation first, when the doors and windows are welded to the wall or framed cutouts, the head generated can burn the insulation material, damaging it and releasing potentially harmful fumes.

As far as the windows themselves, there are many types of windows that you can choose from. Some are traditional, while some are luxurious and are inspired by modern technology. When choosing the type of windows to install, your climate plays a big role. Other factors to consider are privacy, the amount of natural light, and the desired thermal properties.

Types of Windows

Burglar Bar Window: Despite the strength of a shipping container structure, windows introduce a weakness to the security of your house. If you live in a neighborhood that is not safe, you need to be protected against break-ins. Steel framed windows are the best choice because you can weld bars to reinforce your security. Choose a window that you can pull up because you will be welding the bars to the window frame itself, not the container's frame. Alternatively, you can install windows that open to the outside and fix the bars a little inside into the window frame.

Privacy Window: If you don't want anyone peeking into your container home you can install small windows that are located a bit high up above the eye level.

Sliding Glass Window: A small container will feel cramped if there is no natural light coming into the house, and a sliding glass window can open up the space. Sliding windows come in different sizes. They are mostly made of aluminium, and sometimes you can get a custom size if you are willing to pay for it. The challenge with fixing aluminium windows to a steel frame is that the two metals react together, so you will need to line the aluminium frame with a material that prevents the two materials from coming into contact with each other.

Sliding Shuttered: Sliding shuttered windows are intended to preserve the characteristic rugged look of the shipping container and do not include see through glass. Instead, there is an insulated metal sheet, and because they are metal, they provide an extra layer of security when closed. The downside is that, when you are inside the container, you will need to keep the windows open if you want to see out or have any natural light coming in. Also, if you don't want objects to fly into your house when the windows are open, you will need to install blinds that can be rolled up and down over the window. The blinds will do a good job at protecting from the rain too.

Standard Windows: You can install the standard double window that comes with blinds pre-installed. The windows are ideal for living rooms and home offices. The window frames are usually wooden, and may need to be screwed into the wall to be secured properly.

Double Glazed Windows: These windows have two glass panes per panel, with an air gap in between. The air is contained between the two glasses and acts as an insulator to reduce heat transfer between the interior and the exterior. The gap ranges between 0.236 - 0.787 inches (6 - 20 mm), and the bigger the gap, the better the thermal insulation. They help to reduce the heating costs in cold climates, but they can be pretty expensive. For an eco-friendly enthusiast, buying double glazed windows is the best way to take advantage of physics to keep the internal conditions comfortable. Heat transfer can be reduced by almost a third if double glazed windows are installed correctly. Cold climates can benefit from double glazed windows because they reduce condensation. The inside glass stays at a higher temperature than the outside window, and this is a big benefit for container structures where condensation is a major concern.

Types of Doors

The shipping containers come with a cargo door that you can still use as a main door to provide access to the house. If it's in good condition, it will seal naturally, and the locking mechanism will provide you with decent security. You can also add different doors to access the house, and certainly need to install internal doors to access different rooms. The following doors are options available to you.

Sliding Glass Doors: These doors are similar to sliding windows and come with an aluminium or steel frame. If the frame is aluminium, you will have the same corrosion issues if the door frame and the opening frame get in contact. Sliding doors with a steel frame are not a problem and can simply be welded to the container without isolating the two materials. Sliding glass doors can also be double glazed to reduce the amount of heat lost to the environment in cold climates.

Wooden Doors: Installing wooden doors on the metal wall requires doors that come pre-hung with a steel frame instead of a wooden frame because the IBC code requires a metal subframe around the door opening, and it is much easier to attach a metal door frame to a metal subframe than to try to attach a wooden door frame to a metal subframe. These doors are cheap but you must make sure that rain does not get in contact with the wooden door, otherwise it will rot. The standard size is 31. 5 inches (800 mm) wide, and you can use the same type of door for the interior.

Roll-Up Doors: If you intend to have a storage section in your home, you can consider a roll-up door also known as overhead doors. Unlike cargo doors, they open from underneath and roll at the top. Since they are metal, they can be easily welded to the steel frame installed after cutting the hole. It is advisable to purchase doors that have an outside frame already installed for easy installation.

Personnel Doors: Personnel doors are made of steel and welded to the container's wall for a permanent fix. Usually they come with a steel frame already installed, and have an insulated core. They are one of the most secure doors out there, and you can enhance the security of the home by adding a magnetic lock or keypad.

Step 10: Frame the Interior

There are various materials that you can use to frame the interior to support the walls and house your insulation. Wood, aluminium, and steel strips are commonly used. The first step is to place corrugation inserts to close the channel profiles from the container walls. While they are optional, inserts will make insulating very easy if you are using spray foam. Some people skip framing altogether for single unit containers that do not have rooms. Products like InSoFast EPS insulating foam panels are ideal to use if you decide to skip framing because they can stick directly to the container walls after applying adhesive. While it's an innovative product, I do not advise this because framing adds additional support for electrical cables and plumbing.

Metal frames increase structural integrity, but are difficult to work with, especially when it comes to insulating the house. Metal frames also cost significantly more than wooden frames. People prefer to use wooden frames because they are easier to install, and basic tools can be used for cutting and joining the wooden pieces.

CHAPTER 7
MAKING YOUR HOME COMFORTABLE

You need to enjoy your shipping container home. This largely depends on the internal living conditions throughout the year. By insulating and ventilating the container, you can regulate the internal conditions of your home adequately. Insulation reduces the amount of heat lost to or gained from the outside environment. Ventilation is equally important, so you must not close the ventilation holes with insulation. In some cases, it is required to install mechanical ventilation. The units can be installed after the walls are built, but the holes should be cut when cutting the window and door openings. Additionally, air conditioning units can be used to regulate the temperature inside the house. The methods work hand in hand in extreme climates, but insulation and ventilation must be prioritized over air conditioning.

Step 11: Install Insulation

Insulation deserves a lengthy discussion because of the impact it has on climate control. Heat is transferred between the container and the environment through conduction, convection, and radiation. Insulation helps reduce the heat losses from conduction and convection currents. To reduce losses from radiation, you will have to block the losses, because insulating is not effective for radiation heat losses. There have been attempts to develop coatings and paints that help to block the radiation from the sun. Radiation can also be a problem at night. A phenomenon known as passive radiation cooling can occur on a clear night. This results in the container losing more heat than it gained from the sun during the day.

The energy losses in uninsulated homes are staggering. In winter, up to 35 percent of heat can be lost, and the same amount of heat can be gained in the summer months (Foilboard, n.d.). Heat is lost through the roof, walls and windows. While air conditioners are available to regulate the conditions inside the home, insulation will save on energy costs, making it an eco-friendly and economic idea. If you can find and afford a reefer, buying one is a terrific idea since it is already insulated.

If you're going to buy a standard shipping container that is not insulated, here are some things to keep in mind. The shallow depth of the corrugated walls creates problems when it comes to the application of insulation. For this reason, a wooden frame is necessary to hold the insulation if it is installed internally. However, you should avoid leaving conductive material such as metal framing studs in contact with the exterior wall if you want your insulation to be effective in reducing heat lost to the environment. Materials that are in contact with the external wall create a thermal bridge, and bare metal surfaces linking the inside and the outside wall will reduce the effectiveness of the insulation material.

Insulation materials also perform different functions. Most have both thermal and acoustic insulation properties. The codes are specific to the thermal insulation only, and acoustic insulation is perceived as an added benefit in a noisy environment. Each material has a thermal property known as the R-value that must be matched with the R-values specified in the code. R-values are used to rate an insulator's ability to resist the flow of heat, just like how resistors are measured in Ohms.

The higher the R-value, the more effective the insulator is and this value ranges between 1.5 and 7. Since the flow of heat is a two way street, each insulator has an up R-value and a down R-value. The former is a measure of the insulator's efficiency at keeping heat inside a building, and is also known as the winter R-value. The down R-value indicates the insulator's resistance to heat entering a building from the outside, and this is sometimes referred to as the summer R-value.

There are many insulation materials available for shipping containers and choosing the right one requires you to consider the cost, surrounding conditions, and climate.

Interior vs Exterior Insulation

External insulation is appealing in some cases because insulation installed inside reduces the amount of living space available, and opting to insulate the outside will maximize the space inside the home. Other benefits of installing external insulation include the removal of the rugged look that is characteristic of shipping container homes. Cladding or wood is often used to cover up the insulation to protect it from the outside environment. I've seen it done in some builds, and I personally found it unattractive and at odds with the true spirit of cargotecture.

This is also an expensive way to insulate your home for several reasons. External insulation is difficult to install and requires a professional job for it to be effective. This increases the cost and you may have to replace it regularly because it is exposed to the outside environment. Rain and sunlight can degrade the insulation making it less effective and porous over time. Once the external insulation gets damaged, the interior walls are affected too, adding to the maintenance costs. Given the issues surrounding external insulation, I always advise my clients to go for internal insulation, and find alternative ways to maximize the interior space. I will share some tips with you on space utilization in the later chapters. I have listed the factors to consider when choosing the type of insulation to install.

Size of Container: The size of your build will affect the cost of insulation. Spray foam insulation is effective but costs more than bulk insulation made from materials such as glass wool and paper. When it comes to insulation, the saying *"You get what you pay for"* is true. Insulation with good expansion properties is recommended, but it comes with a hefty price. In the long run, it will serve you well because of the savings in energy costs for heating or cooling your home in unbearable climates.

Eco-Friendliness: There are two types of insulation—natural and manmade insulation. Natural products are sustainable compared to manmade insulation such as spray foam which has been linked to negative health outcomes such as asthma and lung damage. However, natural does not necessarily mean eco-friendly, because some natural materials are treated with chemicals to give them insulating properties comparable to manmade materials. While materials such as wool and cellulose are natural and can be used as insulators, usually they are laced with chemicals meant for fire retardation. If you choose these materials, be sure to check the chemical composition of the fire retardant used.

Climate: If you are located in a cold climate, you must choose an insulator that has a high winter R-value. Australians might have to consider insulators that have a high summer R-value for their shipping container homes, because of the hot climate. In such regions, reflective insulation is a good choice that can be lined in the walls, floor, and roof. It is a good medium to block radiation from the sun, and material made from aluminium is a good pick. On the contrary, people living on the coast in Southern California are considered to enjoy an ideal climate, and may not need to insulate their homes at all, even though they may still be required to do so by building codes.

Effects of Condensation: The wall temperature of the shipping container changes with the outside conditions. If the wall temperature falls below the dew point of the inside air, condensation occurs. The air will not be able to hold the moisture it naturally contains as vapor, and liquid water forms. This happens at the dew point of the air. Condensation is the leading cause of the development of rust, mold, and mildew. Insulation that has no moisture absorbing properties can rot because of the effects of condensation. If you plan to build the container home in a cold or wet climate, you must choose insulation that reduces the effects of condensation with good resistance to moisture.

Natural Types of Insulation

Cotton: With a total R-value of 3.5 for each inch of thickness, it is similar to fiberglass in terms of effectiveness, but it's required to be treated with boric acid so that it meets the fire retardation requirements of building codes. Since cotton is a natural product, it is free from volatile organic compounds (VOCs). While it has the advantage of being a natural product, it requires a vapor barrier to prevent it from becoming damp. If moisture gets into the insulation, it will become dense, resulting in reduced effectiveness and possibly mold.

Wool: Sourced from sheep,it has the same R-value as cotton. Its biggest advantage is that it contains lanolin which is a natural fire retardant chemical. There is no need for wool to be additionally treated. Compared to cotton, it can absorb just over a third of its weight in water with little impact on its thermal properties because of the hygroscopic fibers. Using wool is not recommended unless it is treated with anti corrosion. If untreated, it can lead to the material's deterioration or fail to reduce condensation inside the walls. Apart from this, it is usually laced with chemicals meant for fire retardation. If you choose this material, be sure to check the chemical composition of the fire retardant used.

Cork: This is one of the most eco-friendly insulation materials. It's made from tree bark, meaning that trees will not be cut to produce it. Cork is renewable since it can be harvested every nine years from the same tree and is biodegradable as well. In addition to its thermal properties, it also acts as a sound barrier and can be used to soundproof your home from outside noise. Cork is a good candidate to be used as installation in warmer climates in a shipping container home. It can still be used in colder climates, but it will need to be thicker to achieve high enough R-values and you'll need to install a vapor barrier between the cork and the container walls.

Artificial Insulation

Spray Foam: Using spray foam is the quickest way to insulate any side of the container walls. You need a spray gun for this job. Apart from the quick application process, spray foam reduces off-gas entering your home because it traps the VOCs. From an eco-friendly perspective it is not a good option because it is made from petroleum products although the impact varies between different types of insulation. Icynene is the best choice because the VOCs will become almost undetectable within three weeks of installation. It is a polyurethane that is water-blown and quickly sets into small plastic bubbles which act to insulate the home. It is an expensive way to insulate but it lasts a long time and does an amazing job. To complete the job, ceramic insulation paint is required to provide a proper seal to the insulator.

Styrene Foam: This is a basic insulator that is cost effective. Styrene foam is used in combination with plywood for sufficient insulation properties. The foam is placed between the container walls and the plywood, which can be painted to suit the interior design of the project.

Fiberglass: Made from glass that is melted and spun into fibers together with plastic materials, this material is cost-effective. Since glass does not burn, the insulator is a great fire retardant. It is also pest resistant and possesses some mold resistant abilities. However, once mold develops, it can grow easily throughout the insulator. It's major pros are that it requires no curing and can insulate both heat and sound, with a sound transmission rating of 43. The major disadvantage is that fiberglass has little resistance to airflow, and its small particles can irritate the respiratory system if inhaled, leading to breathing problems. It is best used for walls that are roughly finished as well as floor, open walls, and ceilings.

Cellulose: The material is made from newsprint and recycled paper. Paper is flammable, and the regulations require cellulose based insulators to be treated with either 15% aluminium sulphate or boric acid to give it fire retarding properties. It restricts airflow and does not absorb moisture, making it a good choice in wet conditions. Ideally it is best used as loosefill in open areas like the attic and to fill crevices and cracks.

Mineral Wool: There are two types of mineral wool, namely rockwool and slag wool. Rockwool is manufactured from diabase or basal, while slag wool is made from blast furnace slag. If you live near a smelter, it will be cheaper for you to purchase slag wool, and its properties are superior to most types of insulators. It is fire resistant and moisture resistant and this allows it to act as a flame barrier. It also requires no curing during installation and has good resistance to mold development and growth. However, its small particles can cause lung related problems, including cancer, if inhaled. As a result, it requires special equipment to safely install the insulator on walls. It is best used for ceilings where there is less potential for contact with occupants in case of damage to the insulated area.

Phenolic Foam: The rigid boards were popular before new technology led to the development of a variant that needs to be cured. It is regarded as one material that gives optimal thermal insulation in all conditions. The current generation shrinks to about 98% of its original weight after curing, and this might need to be accounted for during installation.

Polyisocyanurate: Available as a foam board, the material is affordable and energy efficient. It has a plethora of advantages which makes it a popular choice with shipping container home builders. With a low heat conductivity, it has a high ignition point of 700 degrees F and an average STC rating of 38. Compared to other insulating materials, it covers larger sections with over 40% superior insulation, making it the ideal candidate for making structural insulated panels, also known as SIPs. On a shipping container home project, panels are quick to fix to the internal wooden frame saving you time and money. Polyisocyanurate is HCC free and more stable than most thermoplastic based insulators making it one of the most eco-friendly candidates. However it's not all rosy with this type of material. A phenomenon known as thermal drift occurs when the gas in its cellular structure is replaced with air when it's in use. For this reason, polyisocyanurate has a short life of two years. It is useful as a general purpose insulator and for open spaces. Facings are required to stabilize the material's R-value.

Step 12: Ventilation

At this stage, you should also consider how you are going to provide ventilation for your house. The choices are passive ventilation and active ventilation. Active ventilation uses mechanical equipment like fans and air conditioners, which can be an expensive way to circulate air within the home. Passive ventilation takes advantage of the natural properties of air. The laws of physics dictate that hot air rises and cool air sinks. Passive ventilation takes advantage of this by setting up currents that cause air to circulate around the house.

Passive ventilation requires air vents to be installed so that when the wind blows, air can move in and out of the house. The air vents must be placed on the container walls similar to traditional houses. This is known as cross ventilation. The air vents must be installed on opposite ends so that when the wind blows, the air inside the house can exit properly. You can also install a whirlybird, or a turbine vent, to ventilate your house naturally. They are commonly seen in kitchens or industrial buildings where ventilation requirements are strict. When the hot air rises, it escapes through the turbine vent and is replaced by cooler air from outside.

Mechanical ventilation is a requirement in humid environments. Rooms that must have mechanical ventilation are kitchens and bathrooms. The general requirements are that the system must be able to extract a minimum of 15 liters of air every second per individual room. There are two types of mechanical ventilators, exhaust only and supply only ventilators. Exhaust only ventilators move air outside the building, while supply only ventilators bring air into the building.

Exhaust only extractor fans are widely used to provide mechanical ventilation, because they are cheaper to run than air conditioners. The fans allow humidity to be expelled before it turns into moisture which can cause mold to develop. This is a big advantage in container homes, where condensation is a big concern that can damage insulation. When installing an extractor fan, mount it as high as possible and on the wall that is opposite the main airway such as a window or door.

Supply only fans suck in fresh air, causing the inside air pressure to increase. This system is useful in hot climates and works together with air vents. Sometimes the air vents are not sufficient to ventilate the house on hot days and the fan helps the air vents to push hot air outside by bringing in cooler air from the outside. Sometimes, your climate will require you to have a balanced approach. You will need both an extractor fan and a supply only fan to adequately ventilate the container home.

Air Conditioning & Underfloor Heating

You can install an air conditioning unit in your shipping container home to help regulate the internal environment. Modern air conditioning units can remove and add heat into a closed space. The units you can install depend on the climate and the size of your container. 40 ft shipping containers have a floor space that is roughly 300 sq ft, and you will need a unit that is rated at 12,000 BTU for this space. For climates that do not experience harsh weather, packaged terminal air conditioners are compact and will suit a small build well. Units with a cooling power greater than 15,000 BTU need a 220 V power supply to function correctly. If you have a 110 V supply, opt for through the wall types rated at 110 V.

In extremely cold climates, an air conditioner might be insufficient to effectively heat the room. You may need to install a baseboard heater if the temperature in your area falls below 32 degrees Fahrenheit (0 degrees Celsius) during winter. They are more effective than air conditioning units, although they tend to consume more power. If you want to go the extra mile, underfloor heating can improve the comfort of your home during the cold months. This is a better option than installing radiators because you can save floor area space if you install underfloor heaters.

The options are dry and wet underfloor heating. Ideally you should make your choice depending on your access to electricity. If you are building your home off-grid, a wet underfloor heating system is better suited for this application compared to a dry electric system. The reason is that electric underfloor heating systems consist of heating elements that do not work well with solar installations. Wet underfloor heating uses hot water that flows through a pipe below the floor. The pipe is continuous, and installed in a manner that results in even heat distribution. You can install any type of floor over the underfloor heating system, but make sure that a thermal engineer determines the system requirements. Underfloor heating is ideal for large open spaces, and you can either install buried underfloor heating or surface underfloor heating. Both options are available to electric and wet underfloor heating systems, although surface mounted options are more expensive. If you are keeping the original container floor, choose a surface mounted installation. It only adds 0.6 inches (1.5 cm) to the floor height. buried installations are better suited for new floor installations because they require the floor to be removed.

CHAPTER 8
FIXTURES AND FITTINGS

The next step in the build is to install the fittings that run behind the wall. This includes the electrical cables and water pipes.

Step 13: Install Plumbing and Electrical Cables

Installing the plumbing pipes and electrical cable should follow insulating the container home. If you are connecting to the main utility supply, you need to make sure that your plumbing, sewer, and electrical installations are compatible with the existing installations.

Some builders prefer to install the electrical wiring and water lines above the drywall to make potential repairs easy to carry out, but in my opinion, the finish is a bit unsightly. In the spirit of minimalism, placing your utility installations between the wall and the insulation looks neater and will not make a small build look cluttered.

Plumbing

You can choose to install PVC piping, copper, or PEX to run your water lines. Copper pipes will need soldering, and if your soldering skills are not on point, rather choose PEX tubing for your plumbing. Run the piping along the wooden frame to support the pipework.

On average, copper pipes cost 64% more than PEX pipes, and significantly more than PVC pipes. Although PEX and PVC are cheaper, there are several other considerations you must make before choosing the material.

Water: The lifespan of copper pipes is adversely affected by acidic water. Since copper is a metal, acidic water can corrode the pipes especially at the joints, reducing its life from the expected 70 years. On the other hand, PEX doesn't do well if hot water is frequently used. While it is expected to last up to 50 years, hot water can weaken the structure of the material, causing it to fail in less time. If you want to stick to copper pipes and plan on using well or borehole water, have the water tested for acidity by your local council.

Labor: Copper is rigid and comes in specific lengths. It must be cut to size to allow it to bend to get to your showers, taps, sinks, and the water distribution panel. This translates to longer man-hours to install a copper water line. Similar to copper, PVC pipes also need to be cut to size and need connections using bends, elbows, and T-connections which are fastened by PVC glue.

PEX is flexible and does not need to be cut or joined to connect the water faucets to the distribution box. It provides for a central shut-off system making it a convenient choice for DIY builds.

Fixtures like showers and tubs have shut-off valves located behind the access panels, and some valves are a pain to access. If you use PEX, each fixture's pipe connects directly to the distribution, allowing you to turn off water for each fixture in case there is a problem that requires a particular fixture to be isolated. PEX also comes with quick connect fittings and you can choose to use crimps or clamps to connect the pipe to fixtures. Only two connections are required to connect one fixture to the distribution box.

Compatibility and Eco-Friendliness: If you are connecting it directly to metal pipes from the local authority's water network, it will be easy to make this connection with PEX pipes. This is because unlike PVC, PEX is compatible with other metal pipes. However, should you need to replace the pipes in the future, PVC pipes are easy to recycle and accepted by most recycling companies. You won't be able to recycle PEX pipes, and they will need to be discarded.

Conditions: The climatic conditions also have an impact on the choice of plumbing material. In regions that are prone to freezing, copper piping is not a good option, because the pipes can freeze and break, leaving you with a flooded mess. You will have to regularly replace the pipe or make repairs. PEX would be the best choice if you are building your home in freezing conditions, because it expands to accommodate freezing water and will not break. Of course, insulation will reduce freezing of your pipes, but there is always a risk that a poor insulation job can leave your pipes vulnerable.

PEX may also be a better choice because the building codes limit the use of PVC pipes to 140 degrees F. The reason is that PVC pipes soften in hot conditions and this causes the joints to weaken, resulting in leaks. You might want to consider CPVC or PEX for hot water lines for the kitchen and bathroom. PEX is sold as blue and red tubes, which represent the cold and hot water lines. The CPVC option is a good alternative because the material has a higher chlorine content because of the free radical chlorination process during its manufacture. Whatever you choose, stick to one material for your plumbing to eliminate incompatibility with pipe pressure ratings and line temperature.

CHAPTER 9
GETTING CONNECTED

You have to apply for utilities if you are connecting to the utility services sometime before you finish your build. The lead times vary between different utility companies, so getting the ball rolling early is advisable. Sometimes, inspectors may want to see the connections before they can sign-off on a project.

Electrical Installation

There are two types of power systems, namely alternating current (AC) and direct current (DC). AC is a high voltage low current form of electricity, while DC is a low voltage high current form of electricity. If you connect to the grid, your system will be AC, while an off-grid solar or wind system will be DC. The regulations discussed are for three-wire single phase AC connections.

In the US, the National Electric Standards are used while other countries have their own versions of National Electrical Standards. Shipping container homes have stricter electrical standards because they are made of metal, a great conductor of electricity. Some differences from the requirements for traditional houses include the cabling requirements. Traditional houses are wired using non-metallic sheathed cables for lights. A damaged non-metallic cable is surrounded by insulators, particularly wood inside the roof and if a short-circuit occurs, a blown fuse will make the circuit open again. There is little chance of electrocution. But a shipping container home will conduct electricity risking a fire by developing hotspots. Overloading conditions will lead to risks of electrocution if the bare wire gets into contact with the container walls. Both on-grid and off-grid installations are regulated and some local councils expand their requirements for them.

Grid Connected Homes

Considerations include specification on the wiring of interior electrical cables, the method of connection to the power grid, and the method of connecting the house to the earth to prevent electrical shocks for occupants. To get connected, apply to the appropriate offices in your country. You may be asked to include the site plan detailing the intended location of the meter, and consent forms if the new connection needs to pass through private property. The electricity must be connected to the grid before a meter can be installed. Certified electricians are required to connect to the grid for the local authority to sign off. The distribution company is responsible for installing the meter usually on the exterior of the house. The meters must be visible to ensure that their integrity is not compromised. In the UK, you can expect to pay around £1,600 pounds for a new connection if you are close enough to the grid. In the US, the costs can get up to $1,000, while the costs for connecting in Canada average $1,100. Getting a standard connection in Australia starts from $1,320 plus application costs.

Interior Wiring

While traditional houses require conduits to be used to route the current carrying wires, the codes do not require conduits to be used as a protection for electrical wires that run inside the container home. Good engineering practice, however, guides many electricians when wiring the inside of container homes and most use conduits to route the electrical cables. The advantage of conduits is that they make it easy to replace broken wires. Documenting the conduit route prevents wires from being damaged when drilling into the drywall to place fixtures, and the conduit itself offers protection from mechanical damage. If you decide to install conduit, choose the grey schedule 80 PVC pipes, designed to carry electrical cabling. Remember that condensation can be a problem in cold climates if there is no suitable insulation and ventilation. PVC conduits protect the electrical wiring from moisture and are most suited to walls that use blanket-type and spray foam insulation. Other additional requirements that local authorities require for the use of NM-type cables such as Romex include the following.

Wire Location: The wires must be placed not less than one and a quarter inch from the face of the interior wall, otherwise a metal plate must be fastened over the cable route to protect from damage from nails and screws.

Wire Routing: If the wires pass through metal holes, sleeves must be used to prevent the wires from getting cut by sharp edges.

Security: The wires must be secured every four and a half feet and within eight feet of light switches and other boxes. They must be secured in enclosed areas and should not be exposed under any circumstances. Adhesive foam with expansive properties is desirable to secure the wires if they cannot be fastened using regular clamps.

Exterior Wiring

If you are building a shipping container home within an existing residential home, you can draw power from the existing connection's main distribution board to the container using an underground cable. Temporary and DIY connections can use cables neatly tucked away to avoid accidents. Using an appropriately rated cable running between posts is highly recommended. It is important that the cable does not have joints in order to reduce electrical accidents should the cable separate. Such connections consider the existing house as the source and the container home as the load. Socket connections must be waterproof and suitable for outdoor use, and the source socket must be fitted with a Residual Current Device (RCD) for protection.

If the container home is considered a permanent structure, the recommendation is to place the wire underground. You will need to dig a trench and house the cable in non-metallic conduit that meets the specifications described above. The codes require the conduit to be placed at least one and a half feet below the ground in non-freeze climates. Regions that experience freezing must bury their cable carrying conduits below the freezing line. If UF-type cables are used, conduit is not necessary, but the cable must be buried not less than two feet below the ground. It is a must to put conduits at the entry and exit points between UF-type cables and the ground.

Distance is a factor that can also influence if you need to bury the supply cable in the ground. The cables must be buried at least 17.8 inches (450 mm) deep into the ground. If allowed by the local authority, you can save costs by digging a single trench for your electrical cable, telecom line, gas line, and water line.

Grounding/Earthing

Electrical connections must be earthed to prevent electrical shocks. Grounding and earthing are two ways to connect the earth and the power supply, and while it may be confusing, the difference lies in where the non-earth contact is connected. When the opposite end of the cable is connected to the current carrying side of electrical appliances, the system is said to be grounded. Earthed systems involve the opposite end of the cable being connected to a metal body which is part of the electrical appliance.

The assumption is that the transformer supplying the power to the container is already grounded and earthed. Find out with your local authority if that is the case. When the transformer is grounded, the container should not be grounded. If the power source is not grounded, then a ground-earth reference is needed. This is done by connecting the container's body to the GND wire and the earth wire.

In any case, earthing is a must. The codes do not consider natural earthing to be in compliance with the regulations. I have witnessed some builds that consider a container sitting on concrete piers to be an earthed structure. This doesn't work and puts occupants at great risk. Earthing your container requires a long metal rod to be inserted into the ground to facilitate the flow of current into the ground in case of a short circuit. This is referred to as zeroing the container. When current passes through the earth rod, the fuses or breakers will trip the shorted active wire side as well as protect any RCD appliances connected.

Gas Supply

Identify the utility provider responsible for your area to know if you can get connected to the grid. In most developed countries, particularly the US, there is an extensive network of gas supply that is part of the grid. Connecting to the supply will require an application. Your application must be submitted together with consent forms, a detailed site plan, and excavation details. In the UK, the cost to connect to the gas grid starts from £300, while in Canada you can expect to pay as little as $15 for the first 25 meters and an additional $125 per meter. Gas connections in Australia vary by state, costing between $75 and $180. In the US, it costs as much as $743 to run the gas line from an existing connection, while adding a new pipe to an existing meter costs between $500 and $2,000. The distance is measured from the supply to the gas meter. If long pipes are needed, it might be better to have an off-grid system. The general minimum depth of the pipework is 17.8 inches (450 mm), and a certified gas engineer must make the connections as required by the regulations.

Internet Connection

I have encountered problems when I try to use my cellphone in a shipping container home. The steel structure interferes with cell signals and wifi does not work properly. The challenges to cell reception are difficult to navigate, and you might have to consider a hardwire line if you make frequent phone calls inside the home. The wifi challenges can be fixed either by choosing the correct connection, or adapting an existing connection. Usually connecting to the internet in urban areas does not have a long lead time compared to utilities. Still, you must apply for a connection if you want to connect your container home to the mainstream internet service. The options available are fiber broadband and ADSL broadband. Areas that do not have fiber optic networks have to use an ADSL connection. This is facilitated by telephone cables that bring the signal into the house. The difference is that ADSL cables are made of copper. This makes the internet speed slower than fiber broadband. Contact internet service providers (ISPs) to check the type of coverage in your area.

Fiber broadband is connected using fiber optic cables. The main line runs along the streets, and a cable is wired from a connection point directly into the home. You will need the fiber cable which the ISP provides and a router, which you may have to buy depending on the service provider. Fiber broadband is faster and more reliable than other forms of internet connections, and there is no interference from the metal structure because the line feeds directly inside the container. In the UK, the biggest service providers are BT Openreach and Virgin. Canadians can try Shaw Communications and Rogers Cable to get a quote, while Australians can approach Superloop and Telstra to check for coverage for fiber broadband. In the US, Verizon and Xfinity are among the popular service providers.

If you are simply adding a container to an existing home, you can use the connection you already have. A wifi extender might be required if you are out of the signal's range. Alternatively, if the container's structure is interfering with the signal from the main house, you can run an ethernet cable from your router to the container and connect it to another router to get a connection inside the container home. This is a simple plug and play setup, and you can get ethernet cables that are upto 328 ft (100 m) long. Longer cables are not recommended, because the signal attenuates, becoming weaker as the length increases. Data cables are rated and you must determine the distance before choosing a cable. Cat7 cables offer speeds up to 100 Gbps, which drops to 10 Gbps after 49 ft (15 m). Extenders help to boost the speed in case you have to run a long cable to the container. Avoid running the cables near electrical cables to reduce electromagnetic interference. You can always use shielded cables if bypassing electrical wires is not practical.

CHAPTER 10
OFF-GRID CONTAINER HOMES

Off-grid shipping container homes can be more eco-friendly than their counterparts connected to the grid if alternative energy systems are installed. When building a container home off-grid, you must consider how to meet your energy needs, access water, manage your waste, and connect to the internet. Eco-friendly shipping container homes rely on clean sources of energy. It is possible to use renewable sources of energy such as firewood, but this is inefficient and may contribute to deforestation. Solar, wind, and bio-energy are clean sources of energy that you can consider using to generate electricity for your home. Local authorities take waste management seriously, and you may need to consult on the options available in your area. For example, in regions where wildfires are a concern, disposing household waste through burning is highly regulated, and expensive. If there is no waste collection service in place, you may have to incinerate general household waste. Organic waste may be disposed of by using septic tanks unless you have a composting toilet that requires no plumbing.

Electrical Installation

Your choice of electrical wiring depends on the source of electricity you plan on using. Off-grid homes powered by generators need to follow the electrical wiring methods for homes connected to the grid, because generators produce electricity in high voltages. Nowadays, installing a generator is no longer popular because they use petroleum fuel that adds to the greenhouse gas emissions. Installing a generator to power your home may lead to difficulty in getting a good eco-friendliness rating for your home. If there is no alternative, consider a generator that runs on alternative fuels. The installation must be earthed as well to prevent occupants from being shocked. You will need a qualified electrician to do the earthing. Grounding is not possible because off-grid electrical installations are not connected by a transformer.

The two leading options are solar and wind energy. These systems produce electricity in the form of DC. In DC systems, the thickness of the electrical cables must be different, and the wires must be appropriately sized to reduce internal heating of the cables housed in conduits. Individual wires with no common sheathing must be used to prevent overheating. When the system voltage is low, current is higher and it's this flow of current that generates heat, which is a big electrical fire risk for your home. Ordinary non-metallic type electrical cables can only be used in off-grid low-voltage DC applications in shipping container homes if they supply electricity to low power devices such as lights.

Internal Wiring

The lower the wire gauge of electrical cables, the higher the power loss. This is an electrical principle and thin wires provide less resistance to current flow. This generates a lot of heat. The length of the wire is also important, and long wires also add to the power lost in an off-grid DC system. The relationship between voltage and current is inversely proportional, therefore the lower the system voltage, the higher the current. As an example, if the current carried by a wire is 30 A, around three volts are lost in a 12 VDC system when a 50 feet - 10 gauge electrical wire is used.

The heat generated will cause further loss of power unless the cables are cooled from the surrounding air. Increased temperatures lead to higher voltage drops. If you are building your home in hot regions, you must carefully design the wiring to accommodate passive cooling. This is why single wires must be used to make the connections in off-grid DC systems. Avoid exposing the cables to direct sunlight, because this can reduce their current rating. The standards provide different ratings for bundled and single cables so be sure to have your system designed before making the installation. If possible, choose the highest system voltage (usually 48V) to reduce the amount of power lost from your system.

Solar Systems

Installing a solar PV system is the favorite method of getting electricity into an off-grid home. Despite wind turbines being a serious contender for producing electricity, they are bulky and difficult to install for the average DIYer. They are also more expensive and few people consider generating their electricity using wind. Solar systems consist of solar panels, battery storage, and an inverter to convert the DC into usable AC. The options are flexible, and with medium skills, anyone can install a solar system on the home. I have listed other advantages of using solar to generate electricity for an off-grid home.

Modularity: Like shipping containers themselves, solar panels are available in different sizes which can be combined to generate more electricity as needed. You can easily increase your power-generating capabilities by adding more panels to the existing installation. This gives you control over the design of the system.

Easy Installation: If you are not a technical person, you can buy pre-manufactured kits that will provide the power you need. Kits are meant for DIYers to install out of the box, and the instructions are usually straightforward for the average DIYer to follow. The types of electrical appliances you need to power will determine the package that you can purchase.

For hot water, a solar water heating system is another eco-friendly solution. The technology is slightly different to the one used to generate electricity. Solar water heaters convert the sun's radiation into heat. The water is heated to temperatures that are suitable for hygienic activities such as bathing and general cleaning. You will not be able to get the water to boil using a solar water heater.

Gas Supply

The major disadvantage that off-grid electrical installations have is that the electricity generated cannot be used for demanding heating requirements. In an on-grid setup, the electricity supplied does not pass through an inverter and can be used to power electrical cooking appliances, water heaters, and other appliances that need high current. To meet your heating requirements, you will need to have a supply of natural gas, biogas, or propane. You can opt to regularly fill up a domestic gas tank, or have a bigger tank installed on your premises. Contact a local gas company to determine if gas can be delivered, which will enable you to have a supply that lasts longer.

You can also consider installing a biogas digester if you are concerned about the greenhouse gas emissions associated with natural gas. Such systems are suitable if you want to take up farming or live close to a farm that can supply you with the substrate you can use to produce your own gas. Biogas burns clean and does not lead to greenhouse gas emissions. While it may not be the ideal solution for everyone, it is the most eco-friendly solution available to meet your heating costs. If this is not possible, you can consider biomass that is renewable and does not release greenhouse gases into the atmosphere.

Energy Saving Tips

When you are off-grid, your energy is not produced consistently. If you are using solar, the power is generated during the day only. At night, this energy is released from the battery storage. You will need to proactively monitor the energy consumption especially when the sun has set, or if there is no wind in the case of wind turbines. You can consider the following to reduce your energy consumption.

1. **Install LED Lights:** LED bulbs are now more affordable because of competition in the manufacturing of the product. The lights consume a fraction of the energy used by filament bulbs, and can reduce your overall energy consumption significantly. Other types of lights you can consider include halogen incandescent bulbs and compact fluorescent lights (CFLs). Always check the energy rating of the product before purchase, and choose models that have the longest life expectancy.

2. **Turn Down Your Thermostat:** Heat is required in winter, and undesirable during summer. If you use appliances to regulate the internal conditions of your home, turning the thermostat down can reduce energy consumption. In modern appliances, thermostats are programmed to automatically turn off or reduce heating and cooling during the night or when a house is vacant. If you can afford modern appliances, consider models that automatically switch off when the desired conditions are met.

3. **Insulate Your Home Better:** Adequately insulating your home will save on heating and cooling costs, which can account for a third of your total energy costs. Avoid shortcuts when installing insulation.

4. **Use Smart Power Strips:** Another trick is to use power strips. They are used to get rid of phantom loads by turning off the power to devices when they are not in use. Power strips are programmed to turn off at an assigned time during a period of inactivity. This can be executed by remote switches or via the master device.

5. **Install Translucent Plastic Skylight (TPS):** It adds natural light through the roof instead of the walls. The size of the room determines the size of the area of the roof to be covered by the translucent plastic skylight. The bigger the TPS the more the sunlight is added, but is recommended to a TPS which does not affect the approved standards of a container home roof.

Waste Management

Septic Tanks: Designed to receive waste matter from toilets and bathrooms, septic tanks are installed underground to putrefy and decompose organic waste. Bacteria is the main decomposing agent, although industrial chemicals are available. The chemicals work together with the bacteria, and you don't have to worry about soakaway water leaching harmful matter into the ground. The materials used to make septic tanks are limited to concrete and steel. PVC is not recommended because there's a chance that harmful chemicals will leach into the ground. If it happens, your groundwater may become contaminated and unfit for human consumption.

There are two openings on a septic tank. One opening is responsible for delivering the solid waste into the tanks where bacterial action for decomposition takes place. The other opening leads to the soakaway for the absorption of liquid waste. Pipes are used to connect the inlet open to the toilets and bathroom. The advantage of installing septic tanks is their high life expectancy. The lifespan will depend on their proper maintenance, and sometimes they may need to be drained by a waste disposal truck. Poor maintenance and use can result in challenges such as blockage and leaching of waste into the ground. Waste disposal companies charge a small fee to drain and service septic tanks if they are blocked. Select a septic tank that matches the size of your household.

Incinerator Toilets: If there is little water available, you may consider an incinerator toilet. Incinerators burn waste using either gas or electricity above standard air pressure and convert it into gas. The gas is filtered and released into the atmosphere. Some incinerators produce ash which is recycled into the ground and used as nutrients for the soil. You will need an incinerator designed and installed by a professional. Incineration must be conducted in designated areas using incinerators which are constructed by either steel or concrete, but before the process, certain rules and regulations are followed to avoid carbon emissions and environmental degradation.

Cassette Toilets: These are small mobile toilets which are mostly used in motorhomes and caravans. Since they have a small capacity, they need to be emptied regularly. This makes them an unattractive choice among container home builders locating their homes far from the grid.

Composting Toilet: This is a system that gives back to the environment. It uses bacteria to compost human waste, breaking it down into matter that resembles top-soil. The product can be used for fertilising and conditioning of the soil. This toilet uses less electricity, it is connected to the solar panels and it does not use water. You can choose from the three types of composting toilets which are separating composting toilets, self-contained off-grid composting toilets, and centralized off-grid composting toilets.

Outhouse Toilets: Also known as a blair toilet, an outhouse toilet is the simplest toilet to install. These are constructed of concrete, wood, or steel. A toilet seat is mounted above a hole where the waste is collected and decomposed. It is cheap because the waste soaks decompose into the ground. This is cheap to construct and to maintain. The depth of the holes are variable, but if you choose this toilet, try to make the hole as deep as possible to reduce unpleasant odors.

Connecting to the Internet

Other than the challenges associated with getting an Internet or mobile signal inside the shipping container, off-grid homes can experience coverage issues. The first thing you must determine is whether you can get a cell phone signal in your area. Internet access on mobile devices has become an integral part of our daily life, and it is hard to imagine not having access to our emails and social media accounts. Start by checking the coverage map of your service provider. Your distance to the cell towers will affect the quality of signal you will receive. This information can be found by visiting the service provider's website. If there is coverage, you can access the internet via your mobile device and use it to broadcast the internet to other devices using either a mobile hotspot or a wired connection. This solution works outside the container home, because of the attenuation of the signal that we discussed previously. If the signal is strong, you may be able to connect to the internet if you sit close to the entrance and windows, where the signal cannot be blocked by the metal walls. There are several applications available on official app stores that you can download to determine the strength of the signal. Weak signals may require you to use a booster to improve signal quality and strength.

Boosters work by amplifying the signal transmitted from the cell tower. The basic setup includes an outdoor unit that is connected to an indoor antenna via the booster unit. The advantage of using a booster is that they work on any carrier. You can purchase a kit and have a professional come and mount the outdoor unit, because the antenna needs to be pointed directly to the nearest cell tower. Alternatively, you can download applications that help you locate the nearest tower using the cellphone's built in compass. The downside is that this solution can be ineffective if you want to connect multiple devices, and your ability to connect is limited to the room where the booster and antenna are located. Other than this, you may experience low speeds that may prevent you from streaming or uploading high quality content.

Some companies provide fixed wireless broadband in remote locations using large antennas that transmit radio waves. You will need an outdoor antenna as well to receive the signals. The antenna is usually mounted high above the roof to maintain a visual line of sight with the source, because radio waves travel in a straight line. If there are obstacles around your house, you may not be able to get a good quality signal. This will affect the speed of your internet, which will already be slower because of the technology used. The outdoor unit will connect to an indoor router that broadcasts the signal to every device in your home. If this service is available, locate the router in a central room and consider reducing the transmission power of the router. This will reduce the attenuation effect if the rooms are separated by the original shipping container walls. If you still struggle to get a connection inside the house, consider using an ethernet cable as previously discussed.

If everything else fails, your best bet will be to get a satellite connection. While this can be a slow option, it is guaranteed because satellite coverage is available everywhere. Fortunately, satellite internet service providers have developed technologies that can compete with broadband systems. It is possible to get speeds up to 25 Mbps for the downlink especially in the United States. Check with the service providers in your area to compare the services they offer before settling on a company.

CHAPTER 11
FINISHING TOUCHES

In my experience, I have found the top down approach to be the best way to put the finishing touches on the interior of the container house. This approach means you begin work on the ceiling first, followed by the walls, and finish with the floor. You don't want to start with the floor then have to do some work on the walls or roof. All the waste from the top will come down to the floor, and you may have to redo some of the work if the floor is damaged.

Step 14: Install the Ceiling

Ceilings will give your home a more traditional look, instead of looking at a bare metal roof. The best option is the modular ceiling, which is held by a ceiling rail. Wooden frames are required for each ceiling module to keep the ceiling board from sagging. There must be a gap between the roof and the ceiling to allow electrical cable conduits to be routed so that lighting can be installed. The ceiling must be insulated before installation, and lined with a reflective material over the insulation to block and reflect radiation from the sun. One more reason to install the ceiling first is to allow the rails to be covered by the walls for a smooth interior finish. You can place some air vents inside the ceiling or just under the ceiling space. The major advantage of using a modular ceiling is that it is cost effective, and the modules can be easily replaced.

There are other options that include a PVC ceiling and frame out ceilings. You can install traditional ceiling boards and PVC ceilings by making sure that your interior frame is made from wood, and the frame covers the roof. This will allow you to nail the boards to the frame. This method is labor intensive and can be difficult because you will need to install insulation under the steel roof first. Gravity can make it difficult to insulate the roof properly.

Step 15: Build the Walls

Once the wiring of the house is complete, the walls can be built over the frame. The material chosen for framing the interior will determine the type of walls you can put. If you use steel or aluminium framing, you can fix any type of wall. Wooden frames are suitable for holding non-metal walls. The available materials for putting walls are drywall, plywood, fiberglass panels, and sandalwood perforated steel as well as plain steel and aluminium.

Drywall: If you want a traditional interior, drywall is the way to go. The seams are not visible after finishing and people might mistake the interior for a regular brick house. It is a permanent installation that will last a long time if installed properly. Its longevity is affected by the insulation. If the insulation leaks water from the outside, it will damage the drywall. Only install drywall if the home is permanent. Installing drywall on a moveable house will lead to cracks that are caused by the vibrations during transportation to a new location.

Plywood: If you seek a more rugged and industrial look, use plywood to build the walls. I often find the material suitable for use in offices and container structures in commercial spaces. The texture of the wood does not create a home-like feeling. The seams are very visible even after painting the surface, but if you want to use it in living spaces, you can install wallpaper over the plywood.

Fiberglass Panels: Compared to plywood, walls made of reinforced fiberglass do not have a distracting rough texture. Although there will be seams, these can be covered by plastic strips. The panels are light, resistant to water damage, and are easy to wash with a wet cloth. The material is resilient and does not crack. It is an ideal choice if you intend your container home to be mobile.

Sandalwood: If you want smooth walls, consider sandalwood. It has great aesthetics and I have used it many times to make walls for houses and container offices for executives. The grain structure is not rough and cannot be seen unless there is close inspection. Like fiberglass panels, the seams can be covered by strips to give the illusion of a continuous wall. It is also suitable for temporary shipping container structures because of its material strength and resistance to vibrations.

Steel and Aluminium: Kitchens can be built using metallic sheets. They are easy to clean, which is why you find restaurant kitchens lined with aluminium or stainless steel over the walls. With an insulating material in between two metal sheets, you won't have to worry about thermal transfer between two rooms. The only con is that they are expensive, and as a DIYer, you may not be able to install them correctly.

Perforated Steel: Similar to aluminum and stainless steel sheeting, the material is robust and suitable for mobile container homes that expect to be moved frequently. The defining feature are the holes which are designed to give the wall better thermal properties while making them lighter. They are expensive, but can be used for any kind of construction project.

Depending on which type of wall you choose you can decide to paint the walls with the appropriate coating. Drywall is easier to paint, and the choice of colors available is wide. You can also choose to put wallpaper over some types of walls, although aluminum walls and stainless steel walls might not be good candidates for that. It's better to leave these walls unfinished. Before you commit to a specific material, ask the supplier which finishing options will be available to you and evaluate how they match with your design.

Step 16: Prepare the Floor

The original floor of a shipping container is engineered, and suitable for use without being harmful to humans. If you are keeping the original floor, it's easy to renovate it without too much work. Before renovating, in order to give the floor a refined look, the floor must be cleaned and vacuumed to remove debris that might have fallen during the build. This will give the treatments good adhesion to the surface. Clean the floor with a solvent such as isopropyl to remove any oil based residue. Apply an alcohol based solvent and wait for it to dry. You have to first apply fill any holes with wood filler that matches the color of the floor before you can treat the floor with paint. Buff the spots that have been filled, but do not sand any portion of the original wood. The chemicals used to treat the floor are harmful if inhaled. After the filling has been buffed, you can choose to paint the floor any color you want. This is a shortcut, and the quality of the floor will be more rustic. Alternatively, you can pour epoxy over the original wood if you want a finer finish. Mix the contents well and apply the epoxy using a paintbrush or a roller brush. Try to work as fast as you can because the epoxy hardens quickly. Begin applying the mixture from the end of the room to avoid stepping on the wet mixture. Most brands require a little more than seven hours to dry. The result is a gloss finish that is easy to clean and does not require polishing. The advantage of using epoxy over regular paint is that epoxy has high viscosity, meaning it can be an effective vapor barrier between the floor and the subfloor. Subfloor ventilation requires a vapor barrier according to the IBC codes.

Other Flooring Options

There are alternatives to the original hardwood floor that can last long enough. Imitation vinyl planks are stylish and affordable. They are easy to customize and you can imitate any type of wood you want to go along with the interior design of your container home. There is no need to strip the original floor. Vinyl wood can be installed over the original floor, saving you both time and money.

Coin vinyl is another great choice that is affordable. Usually a glossy floor, it is water repellent and easy to clean with water, making it a great solution if you have kids that are adventurous. Its surface is engineered to withstand damage from grease, dirt, and acid. Installing the material is also a breeze. It is rolled over the existing hardwood floor, and many people use it for the bathroom and toilet, as well as any other areas where water can easily spill.

Industrial container structures can have steel or aluminium floors installed. The result is a robust, oil resistant, and easy to clean floor. The market has both plain and textured versions. Treads are recommended if there is a risk of slipping that can lead to serious injury. This type of floor is becoming industry standard and many commercial applications prefer to install this type of floor to comply with industrial regulations.

Step 17: Installing the Roof

Adding a roof to your container home is optional. If you are on a budget, you can skip it altogether, but it would mean your house will not be energy efficient because of the losses due to radiation. The best way to protect against radiation losses is to block the radiation, and adding a roof is one option. Installing a roof requires a structural engineer to calculate the roof's load bearing requirements. The factors that they consider are the transient, dead, and live loads acting on the roof. On your part you must know if you intend to install anything on the roof that will add to the overall weight of the roof. Examples of things you need to consider when adding a roof to the structure are listed below.

Insulation: The type of roof you install must allow you to add insulation beneath it to make your house energy efficient.

Rain: Although corten steel develops surface rust that doesn't go deep, a home with rusty spots will not look very good. A roof with an overhang will direct rain away from your walls and windows. This design eliminates the need to install drip bars over the windows. If you are off-grid, you might want to use the roof to harvest water which will be stored in a tank.

Solar Panels: If you will be using solar panels, this affects the roof style, which will need to be angled appropriately to maximize the sun. While you can just place the solar panels flat to match the roof, renewable energy engineers prefer to maximize the availability of the sun by considering factors like the azimuth angle. If angling the panels does not seem practical, a frame can be built over the roof to appropriately position the solar panels.

Shed Roof

Shed roofs are ideal for solar panels because they are relatively flat compared to a gable roof, and with a sufficient slope, the panels can get a decent amount of exposure to the sun at a fraction of the cost. This is because shed roofs use less material and require fewer man-hours to install. The slope is also enough to direct water away from the roof to prevent it from sagging and rusting. The IBC code requires the roof to be sloped at least 7 degrees to effectively direct water to the ground or harvesting system.

Gable Roof

Another option is a gable roof, a common feature on traditional urban and suburban houses. It is characterized by a triangular shape, which works well for draining water and ventilating the roof. Locations that require container houses to blend in with the surrounding properties will need you to put a gable roof over your container, unless the structure is not visible from the outside. Again, local regulations are there to guide your design. A gable roof will give you ceiling space in which you can install appliances like geysers for your hot water as well as the plumbing.

Vegetative Roof

You can also add a green roof to your home. This is the most eco-friendly thing you can do for your home. Green roofs, also known as eco-roofs, are made from a layer of vegetation and installed above the metal roof of the shipping container. You can choose the type and amount of vegetation to plant to create an intensive, semi-intensive, or extensive green roof. This is also another way of reducing the carbon footprint, because the plants will release oxygen into the atmosphere. For a green roof to work, the roof must be either flat or slightly sloped for the plants to grow properly, and also to avoid water and nutrients running off the surface of the roof. The type of eco-roof you can install depends on the load bearing abilities of the roof structure and the type of plants you want to place.

An eco-roof has seven layers below the vegetation. The growing medium is below the vegetation. It provides the plants with structural support and provides the nutrients. The medium is different from the ordinary products for home gardens. Mineral aggregates are used, and a small amount of organic matter is mixed. It is important that the medium is lightweight, with stable chemical and physical properties. Filter membranes are placed below the growing membrane, so that the medium's particles are not washed into the drainage layer. If the drainage layer is clogged, plants will die and the roof will become heavier. Some layers are designed for small installations, while some can be used for large builds and areas of high intensity rainfall.

The drainage layer is used to remove water from the roof when it rains. It is designed to retain some water so that it can be used by the plants. The drainage prevents water from pooling on the roof to promote aerobic conditions. Like the filter membrane, the products on the market are designed to perform different functions depending on the environment. Root repellent sheets are installed under the drainage layer. Its function is to protect the primary waterproofing layer by preventing root penetration. They can be installed on any kind of roof design.

The drainage layer is followed by a roofing membrane support and a thermal insulation. The insulation material can be a foam such as PUR. It's a popular insulation material, because it protects both the internal conditions of the house and the plants' temperature in the winter months. You also get a good amount of acoustic insulation as well. If you live close to the airport, you won't be affected by the sound of airplanes rattling your metal roof. You also won't hear the sound of a hailstorm. In general, thicker insulation will lead to better insulation, but will also add to the weight of the roof.

Lastly, beneath the insulation material is a vapor barrier. It functions to protect the container metal roof from exposure to moisture which can lead to the development of rust if the conditions are right.

Extensive Green Roof: If you want to plant vegetation that requires little water or survive harsh conditions, you can install this type of roof. The growing medium is usually less than six inches deep, but a larger area can be planted, without much maintenance required, saving you money.

Intensive Green Roof: This type of roof provides plants with favorable conditions, and features an irrigation system and a deeper growing medium. It can support larger plants such as bushes. These are good for attracting some wildlife if that is your thing and you live in the right region.

Semi-Extensive Green Roof: A combination of the other two eco-roofs, it leans towards extensive green roofs in terms of cost and irrigation requirements. It has a growing medium depth that is suitable for plants smaller than most shrubs and trees.

Protecting from Rust

During manufacture, shipping containers are made from corrosion resistant corten that develops a protective layer when certain conditions are met. This property earned it the name weathering steel. When it is exposed to water and oxygen, an oxide rust layer is formed on the exposed surface. The protective coating can only be formed if there is a dry and wet cycle. Climates that are mostly wet or mostly dry will not get rust. In climates that have both wet and dry cycles, the oxide layer prevents the rust from going deeper, which protects the core of the material. However, if you don't like the rusty color ruining your build, you can take the following measures.

Protection by Design

Not all rust comes from rain-induced wet conditions. Condensation can also cause rust in a shipping container home. You can cool the home by covering it with a shade in summer. Installing a permanent roof with an overhang will also protect the home from being exposed to rain. This will further reduce condensation inside the container. If you live close to the coast, try and build your shipping container home at least three miles away from the shore. Water must not gather anywhere around your shipping container home. This is a common problem in multi-unit shipping containers that are joined together. You must make sure that the seams are not exposed to rain that might catch on the welds of connection between the frames.

Placing your container home on a full concrete slab might lead to condensation if you do not install subfloor ventilation. If possible, avoid a full-concrete slab. Regularly inspecting your home to check any signs of rust will help you take remedial action if you notice rust developing. You must also inspect following a storm that causes objects to strike the home. If the objects cause dents that distort the paint, the damaged spots might be susceptible to corrosion because of the removal of protection.

Treatment

If you see small rusty spots developing, get a wire brush and sandpaper to clear off the rust. Wipe the area with damp vinegar and leave to dry. Paint to match the color using direct metal paint or ceramic paint to protect from further corrosion.

Painting the Container

Sometimes, the color that shipping containers are painted with are not appealing. After treating all rust areas, you may want to paint the entire container instead of just treating the affected areas. There is no need to prime the container. The layers of paint used on corten steel are already primed for the container to withstand the marine conditions. Check with your supplier, because some commercial suppliers offer a repainting service before the container is delivered. You can send the details of the shade and quality you want to get a precise quote. Metallic and fluorescent finishes will cost more than the standard finish and add to the overall cost of the paint job.

Homes that are temporary and open to relocation must have the data plates removed so that the identifying information is not covered by the paint. If the data plate is missing, you will find it difficult to relocate the containers because the permits to transport cannot be issued without the container's information. Carefully apply heat to peel off the adhesive used to bond the plate to the walls. It's not necessary to remove the tags on permanent homes and painting over them is allowed.

CHAPTER 12
REEFER CONTAINERS

You may be able to purchase a refrigerated container to use as a shipping container home. Single reefer containers can cost as much as $10,000 excluding delivery charges. Converting one requires a different approach, because of the pre-installed insulation. The insulation in reefers must have an R-value greater than or equal to 28, according to the standards. Most manufacturers exceed this value. The insulation material is four inches thick, so if the home is going to be located in a cold environment, you will not need to install additional insulation.

The conversion process you will follow will depend on the type of reefer. Integrated reefer containers contain the refrigeration equipment inside the container. Clip-on refrigerated containers have the equipment located outside the container and feature ducts that connect to the container's interior via portholes. It is easier to convert the integrated type, and this is the version you must purchase if you want to go the DIY route. Look for Non-operational reefers (NORs) if you do not plan on using the refrigeration equipment. They are cheaper to buy compared to reefers that are in working order.

There are several challenges you will need to overcome to convert a reefer container into a home, starting with deciding what to do about the refrigeration equipment. Reclaiming the two feet of floor space occupied by the refrigeration equipment requires you to create an open space within a closed space. Doing this requires the end cap to be cut and moved two feet before reattaching it to the frame. Additionally, you will need to purchase the sheeting to cover the section that has been moved. The costs can quickly add up, and you may find the advantage of the insulation not worth the effort. Other than this, you will also need to purchase and install insulating material to cover the portions that have been cut off. It may be difficult to get the same insulating effect if you are maintaining the geometry of the internal walls.

Alternatively, you can sacrifice the space occupied by the equipment. This means you won't enjoy the same amount of living space that you will get from a regular container. In that case, a metal stand has to be fabricated to hold the refrigeration equipment in place, because after modifications, the container structure will not be supporting it. You will need to hire a professional to drain the refrigerant out because over time, leaks develop within the pipework. The refrigerant is poisonous and harmful to the environment.

Flooring

The floors in a reefer are made of T-sectioned aluminium floors. The profile is designed to allow cold air to circulate underneath the floor. This design makes the floor unsuitable to use as a residential floor. The channels can injure the feet if someone walks barefoot. The options are to strip the floor completely, or install a new floor over the metal t-profiles. However, you do not have to worry about pesticides or if toxic material has been inside the container. Your cleaning process will be less involved compared to a general purpose container project.

Walls

Refrigerated containers do not feature corrugated walls. Instead, the walls are smooth stainless steel panels that are painted on the outside. For this reason, reefers are popular with DIYers who do not find the corrugated look of a shipping container home attractive. The inside walls are usually unpainted, but may be lined with reinforced fiber plastic (RFP) to make them lighter and resistant to chemical damage.

When cutting the walls, it is recommended that cuts are made in a single pass. Ordinary shipping containers have thinner walls because there is no insulation material surrounding them. Cutting the interior and exterior sides of a reefer separately introduces alignment problems and if there is a mismatch, the windows and door will be impossible to fit. You may need a larger angle grinder to cut deep into the wall. Plasma cutters and cutting torches have the ability to cut thick sections in one go, but using them to cut a reefer's walls risks starting a fire because the insulation material is flammable.

Installing the electrical cables and plumbing also requires a different approach in a reefer. In a standard container, these are installed within the walls and secured inside the frame. To achieve the same look in a reefer container, the walls and insulation need to be cut to place the pipes and cables. The installation can be covered with drywall, shiplap or your material of choice. Alternatively, they can be placed over the walls inside the container, eliminating the need to cut the channels. You will need good workmanship skills to achieve an appealing look. Once the cables and plumbing have been installed, building the walls is similar to an ordinary shipping container. Choose a material that sticks directly onto the walls of the container.

CHAPTER 13
EXAMPLE PROJECTS

Now that we have an overview of what to expect when building a shipping container home, let's get into building one. In the first example, I will include the costs associated with each build and the legal requirements, keeping in mind the level of skill required, and starting the detailed process from the building of the foundation. The other two projects will not be as detailed, because the steps required are adequately discussed in the first example. There is no point in detailing the same stage several times. For instance, if the first example details the steps needed to build the walls, this will not be repeated in the subsequent examples.

Our first example illustrates the process of building a 320 sq ft shipping container home using a single unit shipping container. DIYers with no experience building a shipping container home will be able to complete this project without contracting if the tools and equipment needed are available. Following this is a 1920 sq ft off-grid build that is designed to be occupied by a family of four. Some parts of the build may need contracting. The final example project is a two-story shipping container home. This project is intended to illustrate the steps involved in stacking shipping containers.

EXAMPLE 1
Single Unit Shipping Container Home

Design Considerations

Location: In this example, we will use the city of Aberdeen in the state of South Dakota, United States, urban/suburban residential area connected to the grid and main utilities. The climate is cold, and this will affect the choice of insulation, venting, and air conditioning. The state has relaxed zoning laws and getting permission to build is not a big concern. When choosing the location, factor in the position of the sun during the day to suit your individual needs. You may not be able to change the position of the home once the building inspector has passed the plans you submit. Consult a structural engineer to ascertain if the topography of your location allows for a pier foundation to be built. This project does not involve painting the home.

Applicable Design Codes: IBC Simplified Shipping Container Home design specifications and Aberdeen City Code. The R-values for Arbedeen (a zone six climate) are as follows: ceilings=49; walls=19; floors=30. The ceiling must have a higher R-value than the floor because warm air rises. This introduces condensation problems if the warm air and the cooler roof get into contact.

The floor installation will take off a minimum of 5 and 6 inches from the internal height when open-cell spray foam insulation is used. The insulation must be added to meet the required R-value, so you will need to account for the higher interior floor when cutting the openings for the windows and doors. The easiest way to do this is to mark the openings from the inside of the shipping container.

Units: Imperial US units.

Container Home Specifications: 320 sq ft as additional living space for a single person or a couple. The foundation is a pier.

Skill Level: Beginner with general knowledge on the use of power tools and intermediate DIY skills.

Scope: The project illustrates how to build the foundation, container walls, and ceiling and make the electrical and plumbing connections.

Detailed Design

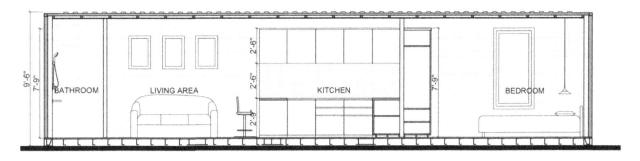

Section A-A

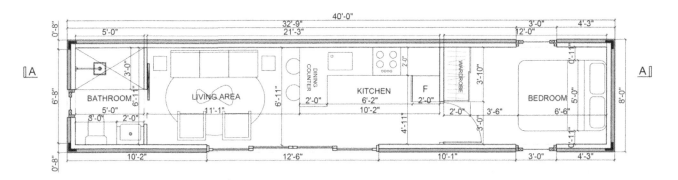

Ground Floor Plan

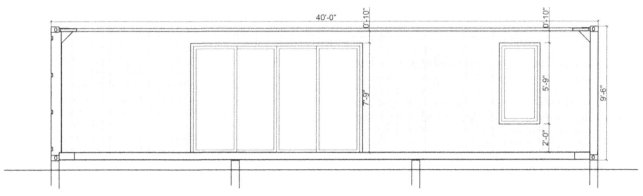

Front Elevation

Project Planning

Description/Activity	Duration
• Permit application, inspection, and approval	3 - 21 days
• Site preparation (assessing site suitability, route planning, marking and staking) • Foundation excavation (digging holes, making molds, reinforcement)	1 day
• Pouring concrete and curing (placement = one day)	7 days
• Delivery	1 day
• Cutting and welding	3 days
• Framing	2 days
• Insulating	2 days
• Building the ceiling	1 day
• Installing drywall and finishing	5 days
• Building the floor	2 days
• Final inspection/acceptance (by appointment)	1 day
Duration of Project	**46 days**

This DIY build requires two people to complete the project. The design has no custom installations, so you can buy most of the tools and materials from a regular hardware store. Complementary activities are consultation with a structural engineer, and applying for a building permit. The assumption is that there are no clearing costs in a well developed urban or suburban area.

Project Materials and Tools

Some stages of the building process will share the same tools, and these stages have been grouped together to indicate the common tools. In the event that a tool is not listed in the instructions, it means that this tool would have been used in the previous stages of the build.

Stage	Tools	Materials
• Site preparation • Foundation building • Cutting out sections	Pounding hammer, nail hammer, measuring tape, square rule, marker or scribe, welding machine and consumables, wheelbarrow, spirit level, angle grinder and consumables, shovel, trowel, drill with mixing paddle, and five-gallon buckets	Water, nails, wood glue, plywood, nine lengths rebar, two lengths metal square tubes, concrete, and ¾ stone.
• Building the ceiling • Framing the interior • Insulating the walls • Building the floor	Angle grinder, cutting discs, grinding discs, jigsaw with blade, pocket hole maker, level, square rule, marking tool, step ladder, cut-off saw, drill or power screwdriver, pocket hole tool	Angle iron, plywood (0.6 inch), timber (1 by 10 inch lengths), two-component Polyurethane Foam Kit (600 bf), batting insulation, vinyl floor panels, silicon, wood glue, two by four inch timber, wood screws, wood, adhesive.
• Building the walls	Drywall tip, impact drill, drill extension, jig-saw, circular saw	Drywall (half inch Ultralight Sheetrock), 1 ¼ inch coarse thread drywall screws.
• Plumbing, electrical installation	PEX water pipe, Romex electrical cable, RV electrical connection socket, electrical distribution board, insulation tape	Cinch clamps for PEX tubing, wire cutters, wire strippers.

Preparing the Site and Building the Foundation

Choose a location that is flat and free from obstacles. Follow the site plan approved by the local authority to the letter. From the design considerations, a pier foundation is suitable to support the container.

Step One: Measure the area and place stakes at the corners and midway using rebar at least 39 inch long. This also works for a 20 ft container, with the only difference being that the piers will only need to be placed at the corners.

Step Two: Pound the stakes with a hammer into the ground, and make sure that the stakes are square and level. If the stakes are not square to the horizontal ground, the piers can be out of alignment with the container base. Finally, mark out a 20 inch wide box with the stakes at the center. Dig out the box slightly larger than the marked outline to have space for the concrete forms. Your final hole must be at least 15 inches deep. Fill the hole with around ten inches of stone and compact firmly. You can easily make a compactor by welding a flat but heavy weight that is around nine inches in diameter.

Step Three: Make a concrete form using plywood. The form must be rectangular in shape, measuring 20 inches in length, width, and depth. It can be deeper depending on the load bearing properties of your ground. The report from the structural engineer will guide the depth of the pier. You can join the plywood pieces using a hammer, some nails, and wood glue. The box must be perfectly square so that the piers can come out properly. Place the form into the hole, and prepare the rebar to reinforce the concrete. The forms must leave a considerable amount of space so that your container is at a minimum height of five inches from the ground. The space below will allow you to have ventilation below the container floor. Place one length metal square tube over the plywood boxes to check the level. If one side is lower, remove the mold and add stones to compensate and compact the added stone. Check the level again and repeat until you are satisfied with all piers.

Step Four: Bend the rebar by holding it with a bench vice grip, inserting a steel pipe and turning it towards you. The rebar will bend where the grip ends. If you do not have access to a workshop bench with a vice grip, use an angle grinder to cut the rebar. Make sure that the rebar is slightly shorter than the concrete form. Weld the rebar into a cage that fits into the mold. You can do this by welding the four sides separately, then tying it into a box with tying wire. Weld the connected sides together to make it stronger. Place the cage inside the plywood box.

Step Five: Cut one square tube that is shorter than the height of the rebar cage and weld a metal plate to one end of the tube. The metal plate must be at least 0.09 inches thick, and can be a circular or square profile that is the same size as the rebar cage. You don't need to be precise about the profile. Pound the stakes in the center until it is flush with the form. Once level, you can slide the other end of the square tube over the stakes that you used to mark the corners of the container. The goal is to have the steel plate rest on the surface of the poured concrete.

Step Six: Mix the concrete according to the instructions. If available, choose premixed concrete to avoid buying the cement, sand, and gravel separately. The concrete must be high strength. Instead of using a shovel and wheelbarrow, you can mix small batches in a five gallon bucket using a drill fitted with a paddle mixer. You may want to fill the buckets first, adding an equal amount of water to each bucket. This will ensure that your piers will be of equal strength, and you can pour the concrete mix into the mold at one go. Pour the concrete into the mold until it touches the steel plate. Tap the outside of the box gently using a hammer to drive the air bubbles out, but not enough to shift the plates out of alignment. Check that the steel plates are level relative to the ground and each other. Leave to set according to the instructions.

Step Seven: After the concrete has cured, get the container delivered to the site. If the container is delivered with a crane truck, gently guide it until it sits on the piers. Weld the shipping container corners to the steel plates. You can also cut some angle profiles and weld them to both the container and the steel plates if you want to go a step further. If you decide to relocate the house, it will be easy to cut the weld using an angle grinder. Your container should sit on the piers as depicted below.

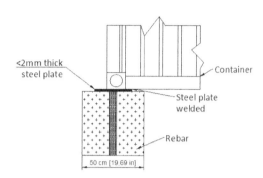

Window and Door Sections

You must have the windows and doors already to make this stage easy for you. Place the windows and doors on a flat surface and mark the outlines on the surface you are working on. Plywood or a workshop table can do the trick. Trace out the outline of the frame bordering the window you plan on installing. You can use this outline to cut the steel square tubes or angle iron to make the frame that will be fitted onto the container wall. Make 45 degree cuts for a neat frame, and tuck weld to hold the frame together. Place the completed frame over the window again to see if it fits. The gap must not be larger than the diameter of the welding rods if you are using an arc welding machine. Weld all the way around once you are certain the window unit fits properly into the frame.

Step One: Read the plan carefully to mark the outline of the cut outs. Your dots must coincide with the corners of the frame that you welded. With a marker, insert a dot where each corner is supposed to go and connect the four dots by drawing a line using a square rule. The dots must connect to each other while making 90 degree angles. Place the welded frame over the outline and check for alignment. The outline has to allow a tight fit between the frame and the container walls. Check the level, and confirm that the measurements from the frame match the design. Remember the measure twice cut once rule. Do this for all the sections that need to be cut.

Step Two: Cut out the lines you have marked using an angle grinder with a thin cutting disc. The size of your grinder does not really matter, but a bigger grinder will cut faster, although it will be heavier. Cut the smaller sections out first before moving to the large door sections. Breaking down big sections into smaller cuts helps to make the cutting manageable.

Step Three: Mark a one inch thick section along the middle of the welded frame's outer faces. The lines will help you center the frames and the container walls. Fit the welded frames into the cut outs and gently hammer them into place. The lines drawn along the faces should match with the interior and exterior sides of the container wall. If your fit is not a tight fit, you will need to use clamps to hold the frames in place before you can weld. You might need a hand to fit the framing for the door cut out, because it could be on the heavy side. Check if the frame is level before welding.

Step Four: Weld the frames into the container wall. Welding from the outside is preferable, because the welding bead will seal the container from the outside. Finally, seal the inside where the frame meets the container wall using a sealer. Ask the local hardware which sealants they have that can do the job.

Electrical, Ventilation, and Plumbing Holes

Step One: Mark the holes for your electrical cable that will supply power to the container, as well as the plumbing and vents. Remember the IBC code (3114.8.53) limits the openings for electrical holes and vents to six inches for every eight feet of wall length that is considered as a lateral force resisting system. Openings located on non-lateral force resisting walls have no limit to the opening size. Openings for electrical cables that are routed through cut steel must have sleeves to protect the cables from abrasion. There is no need to frame the holes for plumbing and ventilation.

Step Two: After marking their location, cut the holes for the electrical cable using a hole kit attached to a power drill or an angle grinder. Small grinders are suitable for this. Grind the opening to avoid rough metal causing injury. For flushing toilets, the hole for the pipe must match the diameter of the unit's outlet that you are planning to install. I prefer to route the pipes to come out from the side walls if I think the container will be relocated in the future. Cutting the bottom of the container is labor intensive and can create problems.

Building the Ceiling

Step One: Mark the level where you want the ceiling to be installed along the inside of the container walls. Your line must be level, otherwise the rail will be out of alignment, and the modules will not slide in. Grind the paint off every nine feet to avoid inhaling the interior coating fumes. Measure and cut the angle iron that will be welded to the walls, and connect the angle iron to the walls using the welder. Ensure a strong bond to prevent the rails from breaking off under the weight of the roof.

Step Two: Cut the plywood into seven feet and six inch wide boards that are nine and a half feet long. You must have four pieces of plywood sheets in the end. Cut 1 by 10 inch timber to make a frame that is flush with the plywood pieces. Seal one face of the frame with silicone and attach the plywood over the frame. Drive wood screws from the plywood to connect the frame and plywood together. Place the four units with the frames flush and measure to check if they match with the internal dimensions of the container. You may need to adjust one of the modules if you notice that the fit is not perfect. Mark out and drill the holes for the electrical cable of the lights according to the design. The hole size must match the conduit you are using to run your electrical cable. Cut and fit the conduit to make it flush with the width of the frame. Turn the modules over to begin insulating inside the module.

Step Three: Use closed cell spray foam insulation (for cold climates) to insulate the inside of the module. The foam must be at least one inch thick. Read the manufacturer's instructions and put on the safety gear provided before you begin. Once dry, add a batt insulation blanket on top of the spray foam to have a hybrid insulation system. You will save money if you combine the two materials. In total, the insulation must be nine inches to flush with the module frame. Since the roof has an area of 300 sq ft, you will need 300 board feet of closed cell foam. Finally, fix a reflective bubble on top so that radiant heat from the sun will be blocked. Turn the modules over and paint the plywood with the color of your choice and wait for the paint to dry.

Step Four: Lift the ceiling modules and slide them into the rail once the frame is secure. The ceiling modules must be placed after securing the frame, because welding the bracket will generate heat that can damage the ceiling. The modules can be quite heavy, so you will need an assistant to install the ceiling modules. Run the electrical cabling through the holes as you slide the modules in place. The individual cables will connect to the main distribution board at a later stage.

Framing the Interior

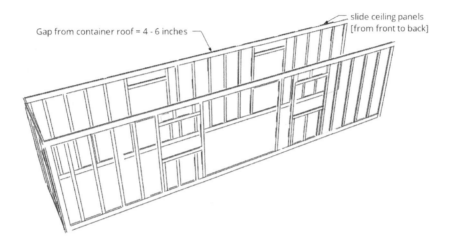

You must have basic woodworking skills for this part. You can choose to make the frame and fit it into the container, or frame as you go. I find it easier to make the frame outside and slide it in. Instead of building the entire frame at once, break it down into sections that are easy to work with during installation. Precision is important, otherwise the frame will not fit properly into the container. The final frame should resemble the one depicted in the sketch above, and the gap between the centers of the vertical members should be 16 inches.

Step One: Measure the height from the ceiling to the floor inside the container. Cut the wood to size, and build the frame to fit the internal dimensions of the container. If you are building the frame in-situ, it is easier to start with the edges and frame from the outside in.

Step Two: Secure the frame to the floor and the ceiling rail. You can weld brackets to the bottom of the ceiling rail for extra support. Make sure the timber is flat against the container walls on its larger face. This will save nearly two inches on each side of the inside wall.

Power Supply, Wiring, and Plumbing

Run the electrical cabling and water pipes along the frame to the point of use. Electrical cabling for the plugs will run along the frame, unlike the cables for the ceiling lights and switches. The cables and pipes will terminate at the distribution box, so it is good to make them slightly longer. The electrician can cut the excess electrical cabling off when connecting to the distribution board. Since this build is an extension to an existing home, connecting to the distribution board is optional. However, doing this will allow you to isolate specific zones if there is an electrical fault. Your power source will be an RV connection that is fitted to the hole you drilled earlier. I recommend running the cable underground even if the distance between the main residence and the container home is short. The connection to the earth must be carried out by a certified electrician to protect occupants from possible electrical shocks.

Insulating the Walls

To meet the R-value requirements for a Zone six climate, you can use closed cell spray foam insulation of R-value 7 per inch. For this project, three inches of closed-cell spray foam are required. The material reduces condensation in cold climates better than any other insulation, and has the most economical R-value per inch compared to other materials for the project's frame. The inherent vapor barrier is responsible for reducing condensation.

Sensitive individuals may need to hire a professional for this part of the project. The compound contains chemicals that can irritate the skin and lungs if there is contact. The cost of a professional spray job depends on the location. You can expect to pay between $1 and $3 per inch of a foot board. The average cost is $1.50. Considering the openings, the side walls cover an estimated 720 sq ft. This means that you can expect to pay $3,240 to insulate the walls with three inch closed cell spray foam installed by a contractor. A DIY job will save you $240 at this rate. If the rates in your area are higher than average, choose the DIY option. Compared to the insulation costs of the walls, the ceiling is cheaper because it's a DIY job, and the spray foam is used together with batt insulation.

Building the Walls

The standard drywall is available as four by eight foot sheets. Install the drywall with the long side across the frame. If your frame is horizontal, then install the drywall with the long side vertical to the floor. Start at the top where you welded the angle iron to hold the ceiling modules. Fix the screws every eight feet and half inch from the edge or as required by the building code. Sometimes inspectors check to see if the drywall has been installed according to the requirements. Be careful to not screw into the electrical cables or water pipes. You must tuck the cables and pipes away or cover them with a metal strip to avoid damaging them.

If you installed the angle iron at nine inches below the roof of the container, you should be left with eight feet of vertical space. In that case, you will need two drywall sheets to cover from top to bottom, and five sheets to cover the length of the wall. This is not taking the openings into account. The drywall should fit perfectly when you get to the floor. Cover the gap if it's short or trim the drywall if it's too long. Trim the drywall so that the window and door opening are not covered. Remember the locations of the electricals and other fixtures that must be installed. Carefully route them out as you install the drywall. Do not make the holes too big. Your wall will look terrible if the wall sockets or shower fixtures have a hole around them.

Finally, the drywall must be prepared for painting. You will notice that there will be a recess at the seams where different sections of drywall meet. For the flat recess along the walls, you will need to put drywall mud with a mud knife. It does not have to be a perfect application that completely fills the gap. Place fiber tape over the mud and apply a second coat of mud again. If necessary, apply a third coat until the imperfections are barely visible. It is advisable to apply drywall mud in small portions to avoid sanding later.

The recess left by the screws must also be covered by the mud. Fill the holes and flatten with the knife several times over until the holes are completely covered. You must wait for the mud to dry between each coat. Mark any imperfections visible to the eye and repeat the process.

For seams that make an angle—for example at the corners—you will need to use painter's tape instead of fiber tape. Fill the drywall mud into the recess and flatten with the knife. Place the tape over the seam, folding it in half so that both sides are covered. Repeat the process for covering flat seams, applying subsequent coats after the mud has dried. Once the gaps are completely covered, scrape any imperfections out with the mud knife until you get a flat surface. Lightly sand the edges to smooth the areas. Wipe the wall with a cloth until there is no dust. You can add a water and vinegar solution to clean the drywall.

Once the surface is even, prime the entire drywall with an acrylic latex primer. The primer prevents the paint from peeling in humid conditions. After priming, apply a coat of acrylic latex paint. You may need to apply two coats of paint for an even, smooth surface. The image below shows a cross section of the final installation.

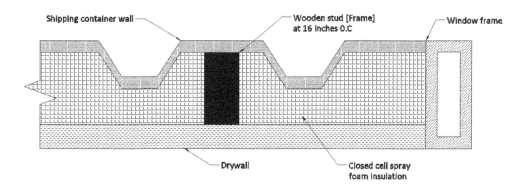

Building the Floor

For this project, the original hardwood floor does not meet the insulation requirements of a Zone six city code. New floor must be installed over the original hardwood floor. This requires building a frame similar to the one used to frame the container walls. Again, I recommend building the frame outside the container after measuring, but this is a matter of choice.

Step One: Build the frame using two by fours and slide the frame into the container. Make sure that the frame is level and square using the tools you have. The frame should be four inches high when it rests on the floor. You can fix the frame into the hardwood floor using two inch wood coarse threaded screws to secure it.

Step Two: Insulate inside the frame using closed cell spray foam. The entire frame must be covered with insulation. The R-value from the spray foam, plywood, and the hardwood underneath will add together to meet the codes.

Step Three: It can be difficult to get an even surface after insulating. Cut the plywood to fit over the frame and drive in wood screws to secure it. The screws must recess into the plywood. Fill the holes with wood filler.

Step Four: Line the plywood floor with the lining for the vinyl floor. It is usually a thin rubber sheet that is sold together with the vinyl floor. After placing the lining, place the vinyl floor starting from one side until the whole floor is covered. The vinyl floor panels are grooved, and they should fit seamlessly into one another. Install a baseboard (or skirting) along the wall to hide any gaps between the floor and the walls.

Approximate Project Cost

Item	Description	Cost
Consultation	Structural engineer/ building office	$600
Shipping container	Inspection, purchase and delivery using truck fitted with crane	$4,000
Site preparation	Clearing (if any), route planning and inspection	$200
Foundation	Concrete, molding materials, reinforcement	$100
Welding and cutting	Welding consumables, cutting consumables, safety equipment	$200
Framing	Two by four timber, nails, other joining consumables	$300
Insulation	Four 600 bf insulation spray kits with two component cylinders and protective equipment	$3,200
Walls	Drywall, paint, drywall mud and application tools	$2,000
Doors and windows	Standard double glazed door panels, standard double glazed window panels, metal framing tubes	$1,500
Ceiling	Materials, insulation, and paint	$1,800
Electrical	Romex cables, extension cable to main residence, RV connector, distribution board and electrician's costs (if connecting directly to mains)	$1,700
Plumbing	PEX tube, PVC pipe for sewer and drainage connection, toilet, shower, connection to distribution box	$2,250
Final inspection	Building officer	$300
Total	Cost does not include purchasing power tools and welding equipment or furniture, cabinets and other fixtures	$16,150

EXAMPLE 2
Off-Grid Family Home

Design Considerations

Location: In the previous example, we have seen how the building codes affect the choices and materials we can use to build a shipping container home. In this example, we will use a hot climate and general design specifications of the IBC. There is no specific local building code considered.

Applicable Design Codes: IBC 2021 Code. The project uses both imperial units (US units), and metric (UK units).

Container Home Specifications: 1,920 sq ft home (six 40 ft general purpose high cube shipping containers). Depending on the soil structure, the foundation can be between 10 and 20 inches thick (25 and 50 cm). The house is powered by solar panels and is not connected to any grid utilities.

Container Home Function: Main property for a family of four. Includes four bedrooms with one ensuite, a living room, and open plan kitchen.

Skill Level: Expert with knowledge on the use of power tools, access to machinery, and advanced DIY skills. Some parts of the build can be complemented by contracting.

Scope: The project only details the building of the foundation, the house shell including walls and a gable style roof.

Detailed Design

This is not a full DIY build project. It will require some parts of the build to be completed by contractors. Like the previous example, the design has little customization, so you can buy most of the tools and materials from a regular hardware store. Remember to buy containers that are made by the same manufacturer. The complementary activities are consulting with a structural engineer and applying for a building permit. The setting is in a non-developed area, and may require extensive land preparation before the building process can start. The step-by-step guide starts from building the foundation.

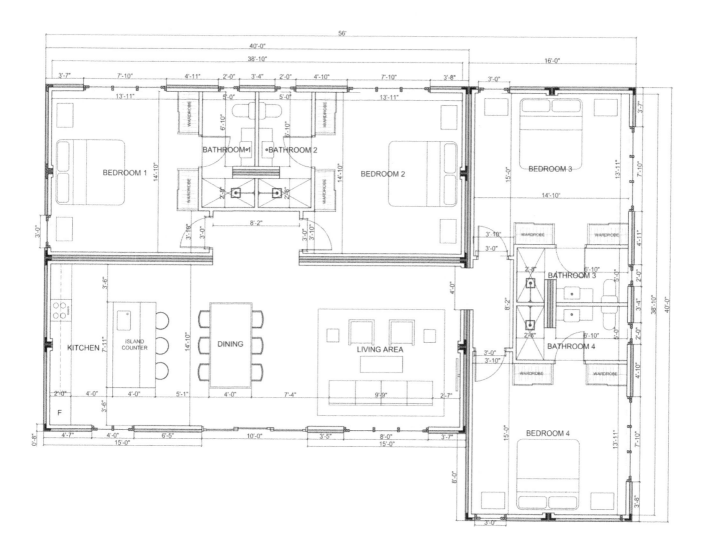

Project Materials and Tools

Stage	Tools	Materials
Foundation	Contracted	
Septic tank	Backhoe or excavator (hired)	Septic tank, perforated pipe, drainage pipes, soakaway stones (three sizes)
Framing	Same as previous project	
Insulation	Cutting knife	Rockwool batting
Ceiling	Jigsaw, screw driver, power drill	Plywood sheets, PVC ceiling strips, adhesive, wood glue, coarse threaded screws
Walls	Paintbrush, paint tray, 18 gauge nailer, circular saw. For opening, tools are the same as the previous project	Plastic sheeting, paint, caulk (paintable), shiplap, sandpaper or sander, nails
Floor	Large roller brush	Epoxy and hardener, wood filler, isopropyl.
Roof		IBR sheets, wooden trusses, 10 lengths angle iron, roofing nails, PVC gutters, solar panels with electrical cables, solar geyser, electrical distribution board
Plumbing	Same as previous project	

Preparing the Site and Building the Foundation (Contracted)

This build requires a full concrete slab foundation to fully support the weight of the house and roof. This will require a concrete truck to access the site, as well as any earth moving machinery required to excavate the foundation or clear the site. Building the foundation will require the supervision of an expert.

Step One: Conduct a site assessment to determine the amount of clearing required. The costs to clear a path for large vehicles and remove big rocks in the vicinity of the construction site are not included in this example. You can start by marking out the layout of the house according to the plan. This will give you an idea of which parts need to be cleared to get an exact quote for clearing. Identify the route that the delivery truck will take and check if the land is stable enough to support the weight of trucks loaded with shipping containers. They might be empty, but the combined weight of concrete trucks and container delivery is quite significant. Clear the site before starting to build the foundation.

Step Two: The thickness of your foundation must have been determined by the structural engineer. Once the area has been excavated, start by building the forms that will hold the poured concrete. You can use dimensioned timber and plywood to make the forms. Make the form inside the excavated hole. It is advisable to have the hole leveled and covered with gravel at the base before the required concrete is poured. The foundation must have an overlap of one feet from the container walls. Insert rebar around the edges of the form close to where the edges of the container will sit. If the structural engineer has specified the reinforcement, this plan must be followed.

Holes for the waste must be clearly marked and you can put a PVC pipe inside the form. This pipe will transport waste into the septic tank when the home is in use. The septic tank must also be excavated at this stage. You may need help from a professional to lay the drainage pipes to the septic tank.

Step Three: Order the concrete. The amount will depend on the thickness of the slab. Once the concrete is delivered, it must be poured into the form. The ideal time to cast the concrete is when the weather is cooler. This can be early in the morning or late afternoon. If the temperatures are too high, spray cold water over the surface to reduce the temperature. The concrete trucks must not arrive far apart from each other, otherwise your concrete will cure differently. Choose a delivery company that will remove air bubbles for you. If the trucks are not equipped with vibrators to do this, you will need to do it manually. Sufficient time must be allocated between deliveries to balance expelling air bubbles and setting the concrete. Cover the concrete with a temporary shade to avoid direct exposure to sunlight when the casting is complete, and wait for the concrete to cure according to the instructions.

Step Four: Schedule the containers to be delivered. You may use a tilt bed truck for this, if the distance is economical. On a full slab, the containers can be slid off the bed into position, although it may be difficult to do this precisely. Have a forklift on standby to move the containers into their precise positions. Place the containers as it appears on the plan.

For this build, there is no need to weld the containers to the foundation unless you live in a hurricane prone area and want to improve the resilience of your home. If so, the container must be anchored using a method approved by a structural engineer. Consider this before building the foundation.

Septic Tank Installation

Before installing a septic system, you will need to check local ordinances for specific requirements. After obtaining the required permits, consult a plumber to help you install the waste disposal system. Once the foundation has been dug, the excavator can dig the hole for the septic tank and the trench for the pipework and soaking material. The septic tank might need to be located close to the road if you are installing a type that needs to be drained, and the pipe must slope to dump the waste into the tank. Place the septic tank into the hole, and connect the perforated pipe to the tank. You can dispose of greywater into the tank as well if you prefer, although this might overload the system. Draining the water into the ground or a grey-water treatment system is an alternative. The pipe must be covered with the soaking material, usually stones that are made of three different sizes to make a filter. If too much water gets into the tank, the solid waste settles, while the water drains through the soakaway. Close the lid and fill back with the removed soil. The final connection can only be done once the source of waste has been installed.

Joining, Cutting, and Framing

Once the containers are in place, the next part of the build is to join the containers and cut the walls to create space and openings. This part is DIY. The containers must be level. The approach depends on your preferences. Some people like to cut then join, but I recommend joining before cutting because if any sections or walls warp, it will be difficult to get the alignment if you join after you cut.

Step One: Join the containers before cutting. It's easier to do this from the outside. If there is no power nearby, you will need a portable generator to run your welding machine and power tools. This can be rented as well, along with the tools. Using a ladder, climb and weld the top parts of the frames together. This is to avoid the roof from potential collapse once you start cutting the walls to create bigger rooms. The roof is heavy, but not strong enough to support its own weight. Next, weld the sides where the container frames meet. Welding from the outside will give you enough light and room to work comfortably. It is important that the seams are welded throughout. Start from one end of the join and continue until you reach the other end. The weld must be continuous and cleaned with a chipping hammer if you are using a stick welder.

Step Two: Cut out the openings in the walls, using the same procedure described in the previous example. The only difference is that in this build, there will be a lot of cutting to do. Cut all openings, holes and venting ducts according to the plans. Always check the level, square, and measure twice before you cut.

Step Three: Build a wooden framing using the same technique illustrated in the first example. This build will frame the side walls and roof. For a large build like this, using advanced framing techniques will help you reduce the costs. You can use either two by fours or two by sixes spaced 24 inches between the members at their centers. When building the frame, make sure the longer side is placed against the container wall. The frame can be built using advanced framing techniques such as using single top plates and two stud corners. One advantage is that the R-value of the wall will increase, because thicker insulation can be installed. In this example we'll be using rockwool blanket type insulation. Consider hiring a carpenter if you don't think you can build the frame on your own. Before installing the frame, staple reflective insulation to cover the side of the frame that will be placed against the wall. Install and secure the frame using brackets at the top and screws at the bottom. You can also use adhesive to bond the frame to the corrugated wall.

Electrical Wiring (DIY and Contracted)

The house is designed to generate its own electricity using solar panels. Solar panels generate electricity rated at 12V. This is a low voltage system, and the wiring regulations require non-sheathed cables. Each wire must be separately insulated to reduce heat losses. Decide on the system voltage before purchasing the electrical cables and consider a 48V system if it is available as a package, otherwise you will need to have the system wired in series. A 48V system experiences up to 16 times less power loss than a 12V system. You may need to consult a qualified electrician before you decide on the system voltage. The wire size and other system requirements can be calculated once the system voltage has been decided on.

To wire the electrical cables to the outlets, start from where the main board will be located. Do this by securing them to the frame using wire clips or wire staples. The wires must be outside the reflective insulator, to avoid touching the metal walls of the container. Terminate the wires at their openings and the main board. Only qualified electricians must perform the connection to the solar PV system.

Insulating (DIY)

The reflective sheeting installed will help reflect radiant heat. Buy a version that will act as a moisture barrier. Alternatively, you can place the vapor barrier above the reflective sheets before wiring. This will prevent the insulation from developing mold and rotting. Purchase rockwool insulation to fit the size of your stud bay. The stud bay is the distance between the vertical members of the frame and the standard sizes are 16 inches and 24 inches. Rockwool insulation is ideal for this build because hot climates such as California and some parts of Australia experience fires regularly. Rockwool is fireproof, and will help protect the inside of your home from a wildfire.

Step One: Gently fit the rockwool batting inside the stud bay starting from the top. There is no need to stick the rockwool if your stud bay is standard. Use a knife to trim the rockwool to fit the bottom.

Step Two: Slice grooves into the rockwool and fold it slightly to insert any electrical cables that run across the wall and roof. The cables must fit inside the grooves. Poke small holes for the electrical outlets' wires of plugs, switches, and lights. Pipes can also be grooved into the rockwool. Be careful to not cut the entire section out when making the groove. The goal is to avoid squashing the insulation. It must be flush with the frame.

Installing the Ceiling (DIY)

Step One: Install plywood sheets under the insulated roof frame. Start from one end of the wall until the entire room is covered. Repeat this for all rooms. You can fix the plywood to the frame using a drill with coarse threaded screws. If you routed the electrical cables at the back of the rockwool, there is little chance of damaging them.

Step Two: Similar to installing plywood, glue PVC roofing strips to the plywood. You can install any lightweight ceiling of your choice.

Building the Walls (DIY)

For this build, you can use shiplap wall panels to save costs. The material is durable, and was designed for quick installations. It has become popular in recent years as a result. In a shipping container home, installing shiplap vertically gives the illusion of bigger rooms. However, this depends on the frame, and in this case, the wooden studs require a horizontal installation to allow the panels to be secured effectively. Shiplap can be installed directly to the studs, eliminating the need for drywall or a rigid base.

Step One: If you want to paint the walls, you must paint the shiplap boards before installation. The gap between the boards is very small, and it will be difficult to get the paint in between using a brush. If you try to paint after installing, the finish will not be smooth, because the tiny gaps left unpainted will show on the final finish. You can paint the wall panels using an all-in-one water based primer paint. This will save you time and money by using a single product to finish your interior.

Step Two: Choose a light color to paint the shiplap. Gloss paint will be easier to clean than matte paint. To paint, place the panels on a plastic sheet and sand the boards. Remove any dust, and paint the edges with the all-in-one paint. Wait until the paint is dry.

Step Three: Align the boards properly across the frame starting from the top. The boards are installed individually, so if the first boards are not aligned properly, the boards that will follow will not be straight. Use the nail gun to secure the board to the frame, punching through the grooves. Once the first board is secure, fit the next board into the groove and repeat the process until all the walls are covered.

Step Four: Fill any nail holes that may have been created during the installation using the caulk. Paint the walls using a roller brush, applying as many coats as necessary for a smooth finish. If the bottom boards do not fit, trim as required and cover with a baseboard.

Refurbishing the Floor (DIY)

You won't need to insulate the floor if you have a slab foundation and the shipping container home is located in a hot climate. The original hardwood floor can be refurbished, but only if it's in good condition.

Step One: Clean the floor and vacuum to remove any particles that might have fallen onto the floor during the other parts of the build. You will need to clean the floor with isopropyl before you can apply epoxy to give it a new look. Isopropyl is the best agent to remove oil-based residue that prevents the epoxy from penetrating the hardwood. Make sure that the area is well-ventilated because the pesticide fumes can be harmful if inhaled, and consider wearing respiratory protection. Once the floor is dry, the epoxy can be applied.

Step Two: Inspect the floor and fill any significant dents and holes with wood filler paste to cover noticeable dents. The epoxy is a two-component system that needs a hardener to set. Mix the hardener and the epoxy according to the instructions. Grab a thick paint roller, and apply over the whole floor. Do this quickly, because the mixture can harden quickly under some conditions. You have to avoid going back to the areas you have applied epoxy. The epoxy must be left to dry as directed, but after it is fully cured, you will have a smooth glossy finish that is easy to clean and maintain.

Building the Roof (DIY)

This design has a gable roof to hold the solar panels and water heating system. The advantage of a gable roof style in an off-grid setting is that you can harvest more water compared to a shed roof or flat roof style. You will need gutters to capture the rain, which can be collected into a water tank. Most modern roofing material options can be used, but IBR sheets are a great compromise between strength, aesthetics, and cost. If you want to install cement tiles or heavier material, the structure must be strong enough to support the weight of the total load. You can take the following steps to install the gable roof.

Step One: Size and weld right-angled steel plates along the outer edges of the shipping containers. The steel plates should be of equal size with the beam that will be installed around the edges of the roof. So if you plan on using one by eight boards, your steel plates must be one inch by one inch, because the eight inch surface will be placed flat against the rooftop.

Step Two: Installing a gable roof over a single container is easy, but for this build, you may need a carpenter's help, otherwise your roof will look awkward. I remember my first DIY gable roof did not look straight and had a number of makeshift wooden pieces attached just to hold the structure together. Attach trusses to the wooden beams using screws starting from one end until you complete the entire roof. This should be followed by installing purlins across the trusses so that the trusses are secure and complete with a triangular shape. The trusses must overlap so that rain water does not get in contact with the container's roof. Attach a soffit board and a fascia board below the trusses. You must ensure that there is at least a one inch gap in the middle of the soffit board to allow air circulation inside the roof. This will help reduce the roof temperature.

Step Three: Fix the roofing sheets over the roof starting from the middle going outwards. The sheets must be staggered, so that water flows from one roofing sheet to the next without leaking underneath the sheets. Fix the sheets to the trusses using roofing nails, and trim the edges of the sheets if they are too long as you get to the edge of the roof. Install roofing ridge caps to prevent water from entering the roof through the gaps. Ridge caps are V-shaped pieces that are angled to match the roof slope.

Step Four: Install the gutters around the edges of the roof to capture rainwater. PVC gutters are easier to install, and are durable compared to galvanized gutters. If you are harvesting the water, direct the gutters to deliver water into the harvesting tank.

Step Five: Install solar panels and solar water heating system. This must be done by certified personnel, otherwise you risk damaging the solar system. Frequent mistakes include incorrectly wiring the system and inefficient placement of the solar panels. The system can be connected to the electrical distribution board to feed power into the house.

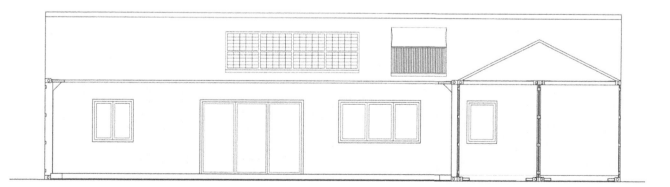

Approximate Project Cost

Like every shipping container home project, the costs to build an off-grid home using six shipping container homes depends on the location. You can expect to pay around $193,000 in material costs and $80,000 in contracting costs if you are chipping in on some parts of the build. The cost of tools has not been included, because seasoned DIYers usually have most of the tools lying around.

EXAMPLE 3
Multi-Story Container Home

Design Considerations

Container Home Specifications: Duplex constructed from four 40-ft containers. The foundation is a full concrete slab, and features an intensive eco-roof.

Skill Level: Expert with knowledge on the use of power tools, access to machinery, and advanced DIY skills. Some parts of the build can be complemented by contracting.

Scope: The example will illustrate how to stack containers without welding, build a green roof, and paint a shipping container home.

Structural Reinforcements: Steel cross beams under the upper deck container roofs.

Detailed Design

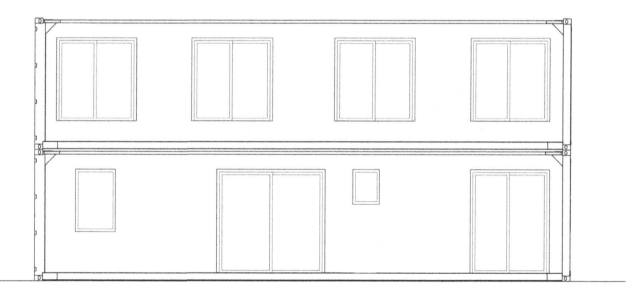

Front Elevation

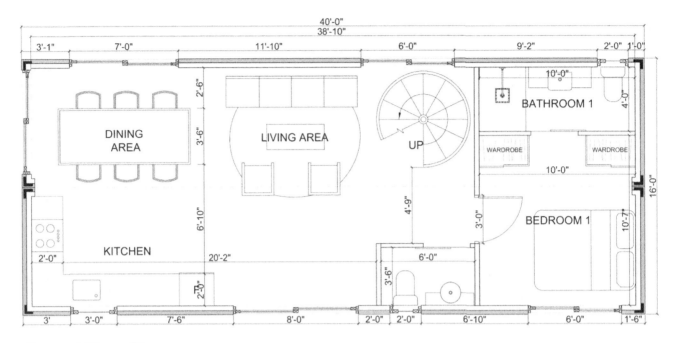

Ground Floor Plan

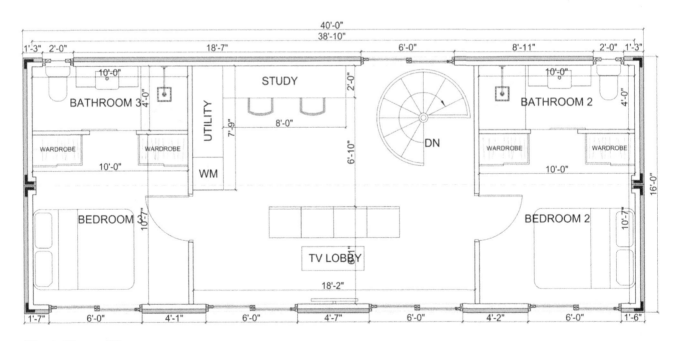

First Floor Plan

Project Materials and Tools

The table below details the tools and materials required for stages that are different to the stages involved in the previously discussed projects.

Stage	Tools	Materials
Painting	Compressor with spray gun, roller brush, angle grinder with grinding wheel	Elastomeric paint, plastic sheeting, painter's tape
Joining	Long ladder, crane (hired)	Twist lock pins for each corner
Green roof building	Cutting and welding equipment	Cross beams (square tubes or I-beams), plywood sheets, wood sealer, silicone, PVC gutters, decking timber, water barrier sheets, root barrier sheets, PUR insulation, drainage layer sheets, growing medium, filter fabric, plants.

Initial Building Stages (Contracted and DIY)

It is much easier to complete the build on the ground first before lifting the containers. This is a matter of preference, and the final outcome will not be affected, but stacking the containers before building may increase the labor costs and introduce additional safety issues. Working at a height will need additional safety equipment and skilled labor. Start by placing the lower containers on the foundation, preferably a full concrete slab. The foundation must support the weight of stacked containers over a small area. This makes a pier foundation risky, because stacked containers exert more pressure per unit area than containers that are not stacked. Full concrete slabs must be contracted for this build. Proceed with cutting the window and door sections, installing the frame, and building the ceiling. Follow the steps illustrated in the first example for this and other required stages of the conversion process. You will also need to build the stairs so that you can gain access to the upper rooms. This is a job best done by professionals. The materials that can be used include wood, steel and brick, similar to how stairs are built in traditional homes.

Adjoining the Walls (Contracted)

If you are using adjoining walls to create bigger rooms, the bottom containers must be joined first. You can only weld the seams at the floor from the inside, because the underside cannot be accessed once the containers are laid on the foundation. The welds must completely cover all the seams where the containers meet, and this is a job you have to outsource because of the complexity of welding stacked shipping containers. The floors of the upper containers may also need to be cut, adding to the difficulty level.

Painting the Containers (DIY)

Once the initial stages have been completed, the containers must be painted before they are lifted and connected to each other. The containers must be dry before the walls can be painted. If you live in a hot climate, choose a light color that will not absorb heat.

Step One: It is recommended to paint the walls after the exterior windows and doors have been installed to avoid chipping the paint off. You will have to touch up any damage if the container is painted before the windows and doors are installed. Cover the doors and windows with a plastic sheet and use painter's tape to stick the sheeting to the surface.

Inspect the exterior walls to determine the areas that need preparation. Your inspection should include looking for rust and areas where the paint is peeling off. This is common on containers that have been previously painted.

Step Two: After identifying the problem areas, grind off the imperfections using a grinding wheel attached to an angle grinder. The grinding wheel must expose the bare metal without reducing the thickness of the material.

Step Three: For the first coat, apply an elastomeric paint using a spray gun. You will need to use high pressure to apply the paint, because the product is thick and a reasonable amount of force is required for the paint to pass through the nozzle of the gun. The paint is flexible, and ensures that all the dents and imperfections are covered for the final finish to be smooth. Roller brushes can be used if a compressor is not available. It will take longer to apply the paint with a roller brush, but it is possible to get a good finish. Once the paint is dry, the surface coating can be applied. Elastomeric paints are elastic and help to reduce the temperature of the container.

Step Four: Apply a coat of general purpose paint using either a spray gun or a roller brush. If the elastomeric paint is applied correctly, one coat of general purpose paint is sufficient to give the desired finish. Remove the protective plastic sheeting covering the windows and doors after the paint has dried. Instead of general purpose paint, ceramic paint can be used if you want to further reduce the heat absorbed by the container walls.

Making the Connections (Contracted and DIY)

The containers must be delivered by a truck fitted with a crane, otherwise you will need to hire a crane to lift and position them. Place the lower containers onto the foundation, and ensure that they are level to eliminate any possibility of the top containers tipping over in unstable conditions. Strong winds are one hazard you should look out for. The OSHA regulations are strict for the handling of shipping containers when stacking, and you must ask the rigger if they are complying with the regulations when placing the containers. Some rules include the maximum number of containers in a stack, and an inspection of the castings before placement. You may be liable for prosecution if a container slips and causes injury or loss of life, so containers should be placed with the crane, and the delivery company should be responsible for rigging the containers securely.

Step One: To lock the two levels together, install a twist lock stacking pin at each corner of the shipping container that will carry the top deck.

Step Two: Carefully lift the top containers and carefully guide them into position. When the container is hanging freely, the rig creates a leverage that will make it easy for a few people to guide the container into position by hand. It is important that the corner casts are perfectly aligned, or else the pins will not latch into the holes. Once the containers are resting on top of each other connecting pins can be fastened to hold the containers together. If a crane is unavailable, hire a heavy duty forklift. The fork lift must be fitted with eight foot tines to prevent damaging the floor.

In the event that the containers are stacked before the pins are installed, bridge clamps can be used as an alternative to the pins. The clamps allow two containers to be fastened together without lifting the containers. To install the bridge clamps, twist the shaft of the clamp until the distance between the grips is at least 7.87 inches (200 mm). Place the clamps across adjacent castings and check to see if the grip hooks are properly embedded inside the casting. Once in position, tighten the grips with the appropriate spanner making sure that the torque is sufficient to prevent the nut from loosening under normal and abnormal loading conditions. You can check with the manufacturer to determine the allowable torque to avoid breaking the nut.

Clamping only works if the containers are connected at the corner castings. I've encountered other designs including top decks that span across the roof of the containers underneath. These designs may require welding or alternative support mechanisms, and will require a structural engineer to calculate the load bearing limits of the lower deck, and provide specifications of the structural supports required. Such designs are complex, and best left to contractors and manufacturers of prefabricated homes. The approval process is elaborate and costly. Purchasing approved models will be more convenient and cost effective.

Building the Green Roof (DIY)

Vegetative roofs are heavy and cannot be installed directly over the roof of the containers because container roofs have no load bearing capabilities. Installing the green roof over the container's original roof will cause it to buckle, and potentially collapse under the weight of the garden. Consult a structural engineer to perform the necessary calculations. Factors to consider include the size of the garden and if you plan on walking over the garden.

Step One: The roof must be reinforced before the ceiling and walls are installed. Only the top containers need to have the reinforcements installed. The cross beams must be welded to the top side rail of the top containers and spaced every five feet to support the weight of the garden. Paint the roof using the painting procedure presented above. The top parts of the roof must be painted from the outside to create a protective barrier in the event that irrigation or rain water leaks from the garden. If you do not want to paint the roof, you can seal it with bitumen and cover it with heavy duty damp proof membrane.

Step Two: After the top deck has been attached to the lower deck, build a false plywood roof over the original roof to provide the incline necessary for the water to drain properly. The plywood must be treated with a sealer to prevent the plywood from rotting. Include an overlap at the lower end so that a drain can be installed to allow excess water to run-off. If the roof does not incline, water will pool on the eco-roof and the plants will not grow properly. The water must drain into a gutter. Place a wooden frame around the roof. You can use decking timber for this. Remember to moisture proof it with a sealer or bitumen.

Fill any gaps using wood grade silicone so that there is no possibility of water entering and causing the wood to rot. The reason for building the frame is to contain the growing medium and prevent it from running off when it rains. The height of the frame must match the depth of the growing medium plus the required layers placed underneath the growing medium.

Step Three: Install a water barrier over the plywood. The barrier will protect the plywood from water. You can use reinforced thermoplastic because it is lightweight and non-porous.

Step Four: Install the root barrier to prevent the roots from penetrating the water barrier. When installing, the root barrier must overlap the area covered by the water barrier and growing medium, and you should choose a material that is free from metals and other chemicals that can be absorbed by the plants' roots or leach into the water.

Step Five: If you are not planning on insulating the ceiling, you can add insulation to the green roof. Overall, the insulation must meet the building codes specification and you can use materials such as rockwool or PUR foam. If you live in a cold climate, the insulation may not count towards meeting the building codes, and you will have to insulate the roof from the inside.

Step Six: Install the drainage layer. This is the most important component of the system, because it allows water to move across the roof after it rains. It retains a certain amount of water to be used by the plants while letting excess water exit through the drain to prevent waterlogging. It also helps to prevent the growing medium from clogging the system, which leads to an increase in the roof's weight. There is an extensive list of drainage types and materials. You can choose between molded drainage, entanglement drainage, granular drainage, and structural drainage. These materials have different applications so you will need to consult an expert to help you select the best drainage type and material. When placing the drainage, the matt side must face upwards to allow capillary action.

Step Seven: Install filter fabric above the drainage layer. The layer is made from textile materials and is useful to hold the growing medium and helps to prevent the medium from clogging the drainage layer.

Step Eight: Install the growing medium. Select a medium that is lightweight and loosely packed. You can visit a local nursery to match the plants you intend to grow with the medium.

Step Nine: Plant the vegetation. Choose plants that are suitable for the climate as well as the type of eco-roof you are installing. If you have a shallow growing medium, you will need to plant vegetation that has shallow root systems, otherwise your eco-roof will fail.

This multi-story example project concludes the demonstration of what it takes to build a shipping container home. I am sure you now have a general idea of the labor involved and the complexity of the building process as more containers are added or designed to mimic the traditional home appeal.

CHAPTER 14
OTHER DESIGN IDEAS

In the previous chapter, we showcased three design ideas that you can consider when building your home. The modularity of shipping containers makes them perfect for almost any design, and the manner in which they can be arranged is limited by your imagination. You may not be an architect, but with a little twist, you can build a home that is stylish. Below are eight design ideas that you can consider when building a container home.

DESIGN 1: **Container Home Blended with Wood**

For some, a shipping container home is just tiny. Additional space can be created by blending the container structure with wooden walls. You need two 40 ft containers butt-joined to the wooden structure. Remember to treat the exposed parts to prevent the wood from rotting.

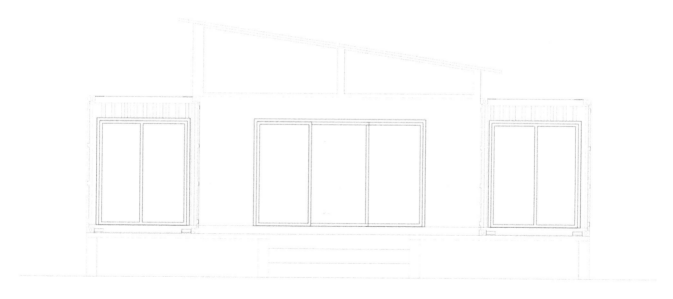

Front Elevation

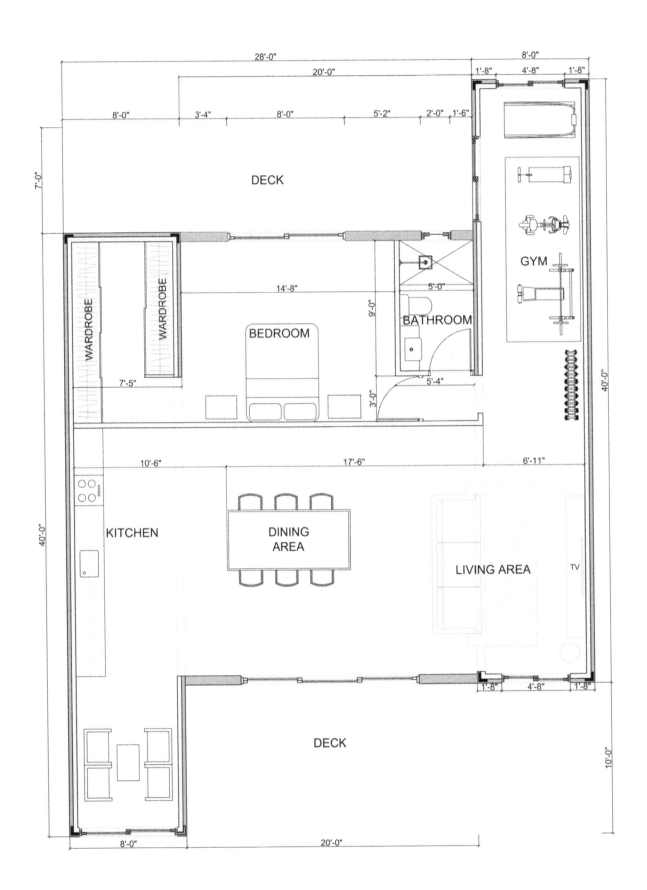

DECK

28'-0"

20'-0"

8'-0"

1'-8" 4'-8" 1'-8"

8'-0" 3'-4" 8'-0" 5'-2" 2'-0" 1'-6"

7'-0"

WARDROBE

WARDROBE

7'-5"

14'-8"

BEDROOM

9'-0"

5'-0"

BATHROOM

5'-4"

3'-0"

GYM

40'-0"

40'-0"

10'-0"

10'-6"

17'-6"

6'-11"

KITCHEN

DINING
AREA

LIVING AREA

TV

1'-8" 4'-8" 1'-8"

DECK

8'-0"

20'-0"

DESIGN 2: **Horseshoe Shaped Container Home**

Kids would love this design. The containers are arranged to form a horseshoe shape that creates a play and barbeque area suitable for quality family time during the weekends. Two 20 ft containers and two 40 ft containers are required to build this home.

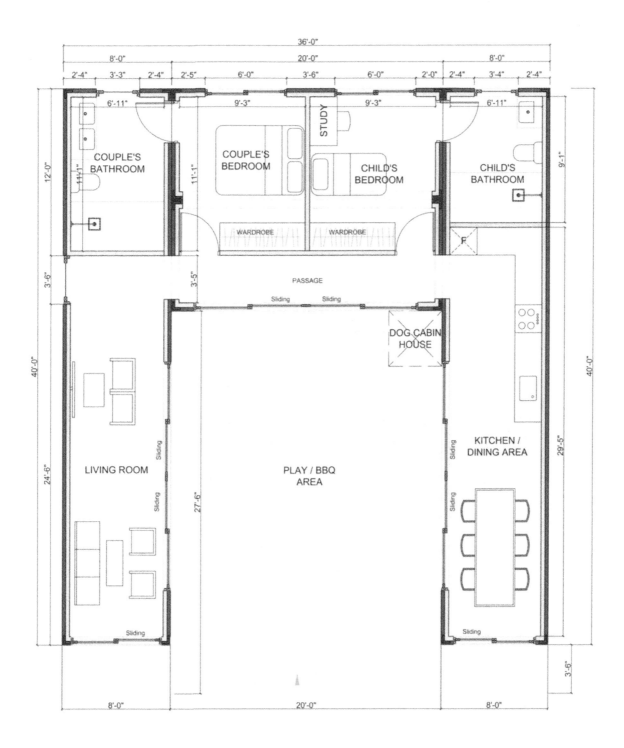

DESIGN 3: **Container Home with Mini Deck**

This design features two 20 ft shipping containers arranged to form a Z-shaped home. If you want to build this home in the city and have limited space, this is a good choice. The small deck provides a tiny space to relax outdoors. Place a couple of garden chairs and relax in the summer breeze. The opening between the bathroom and the lounge allows cross ventilation to reduce internal temperature when cooking, especially during summer.

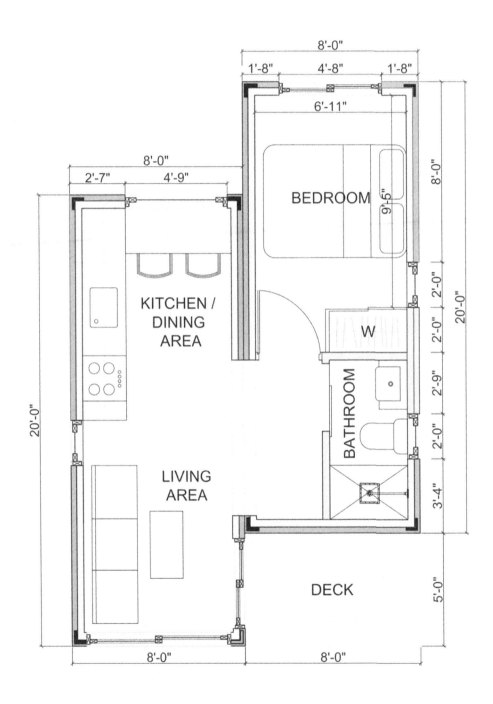

DESIGN 4: **Private Bedroom Container Home**

This is one of my favorite designs. If you ever had guests who like to burn the midnight oil, consider this design. You can easily slip into your bedroom from the outside, while your guests continue to enjoy themselves in the living area without disturbing your sleep. The upper bedroom is created from a 20 ft container resting on a 40 ft container, giving an additional 300 sq ft of outdoor space which can be used as a patio.

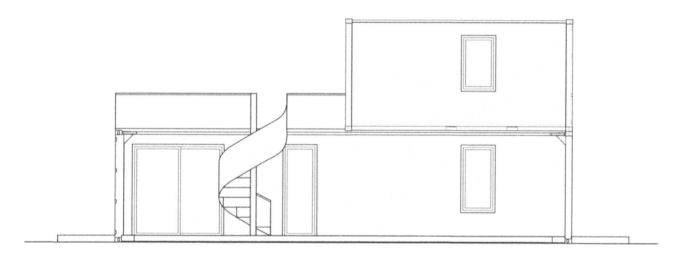

Front Elevation

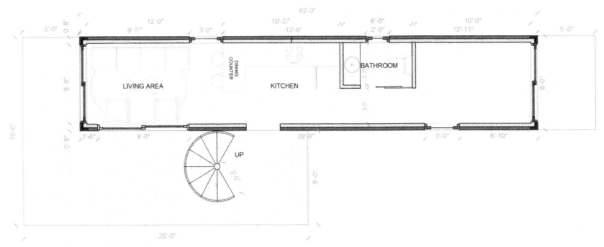

Ground Floor Plan

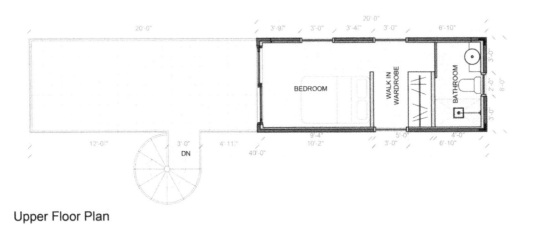

Upper Floor Plan

DESIGN 5: **Cross Stacked Container Home**

If you own a car that you want to keep protected from the sun without building a garage, this design is what you need. The space created below works well as a car park or storage. Make sure the foundation is solidly built to support the additional weight of the car. Two 20 ft containers support the upper deck with cross beams, and the gap between the two lower containers can be adjusted to accommodate two medium sized cars.

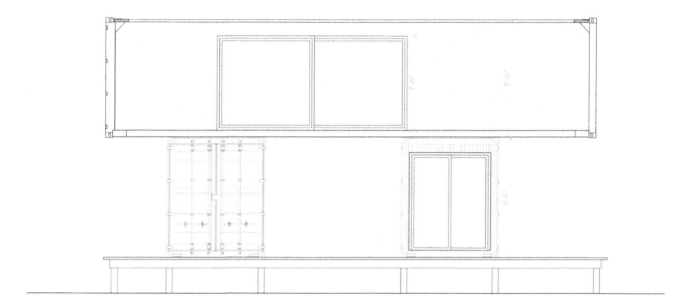

Front Elevation

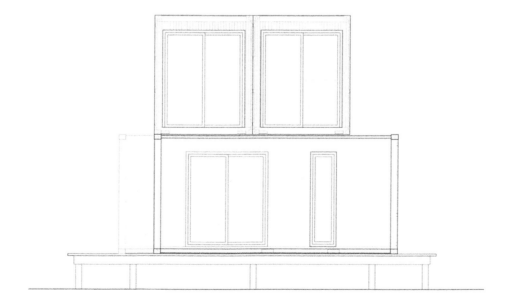

Side Elevation

DESIGN 6: **Open Views Container Home**

If you love watching the sunset, a two-story container home with a balcony will do the trick. With this design, you can easily slip in and out of your bedroom and enjoy a cup of coffee while looking at the views you love the most. The home is made of three 40 ft containers, making the total living space just over 825 sq ft.

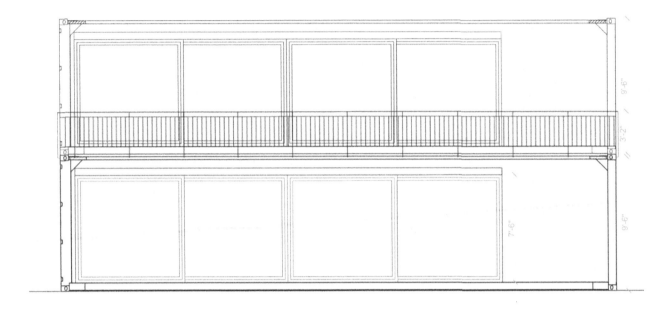

Front Elevation

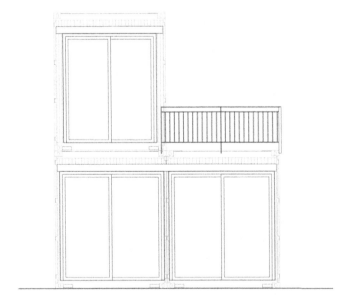

Side Elevation

DESIGN 7: **Decked Shipping Container Home**

We all have family and friends, and may want to entertain them once in a while. A deck is the best place to relax and enjoy other people's company during the summer. Cover the deck with some awning to create a shade and prevent the rain from ruining the party. Using two 20 ft containers arranged to make an L-shaped home, the deck area is 240 sq ft. A great space to accommodate a small group of friends over drinks. Place a few potted plants to spruce up the area.

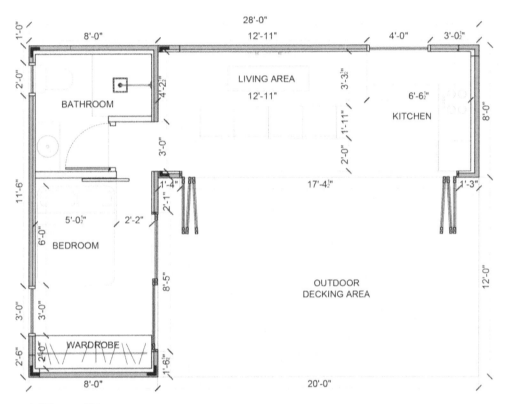

Ground Floor Plan

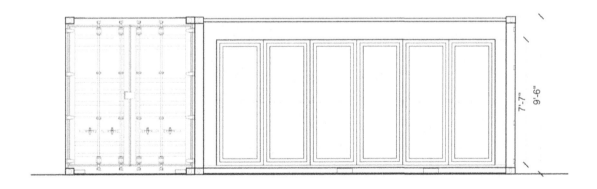

Front Elevation

DESIGN 8: **See-Saw Container Home**

Of course this home doesn't move like a see-saw, but it looks like one. If you have many goods that need to be stored outside, you can use this design and take advantage of the space underneath. Bicycles and gardening tools are things you can safely store underneath. The upper deck is a 40ft container, and is supported by two beams anchored to the ground on either side. Make sure the upper deck is not supported by the bottom containers, because the roof of the bottom containers are not designed to support loads except at the corner casts. You can enclose the bottom open space if you prefer to keep your tools protected.

Front Elevation

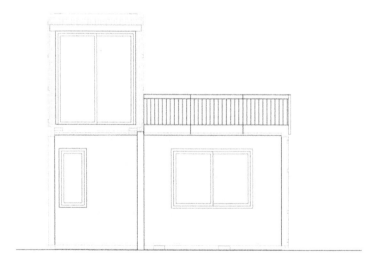

Side Elevation

The design ideas presented in this chapter are in no way exhaustive, but from the ideas presented, it is apparent that the home can feel small to people used to living in large spacious homes. Besides blending a container home with enclosed wooden walls as shown in design 1, there are other ways to build a home that will not make the occupants feel claustrophobic.

CHAPTER 15
MISCELLANEOUS

The obvious way to solve the limited space challenge is by building the home using more shipping containers, but this will increase the cost of the house, and a lot of labor will be required. The philosophy behind eco-friendliness includes efficient space utilization. This is why many shipping container houses try to incorporate minimalist ideas.

Space Saving Ideas

To maximize space, mezzanine floors can be built. A mezzanine floor has an upper deck that is used for regular activities such as lounging and a lower deck that can store a bed which is only used during sleeping hours. This is a common trick that is used in single unit shipping container homes. The idea is to elevate spaces that do not require a lot of head room. People spend most of their lounging times sitting, so it makes sense to elevate lounges or dining areas. The floor underneath can be reserved for activities not related to lounging, such as sleeping or storage. Standard beds also waste space because of the base. Building a custom base with drawers can create additional space to store clothes and linen. You can even consider a full custom bed that is tailored to the physical needs of the individual. If you are short and stay alone in a single unit container home, a custom bed of shorter length can save you space. Buying smaller appliances is also another way of creating additional space. The RV community has been doing it for years. You can find mini laundry machines and dishwashers. Countertop dishwashers are becoming popular, and you can find one on e-commerce stores like Amazon. These appliances work well for a single person or a couple.

Fold out beds and kitchens also help to create additional space. In one project I worked on, we managed to increase the length of the container by using the container doors as an extension of the walls by opening and securing them. After placing a roof over the open doors, an extra 18 sq ft of floor space was created. The extra space was converted into a fold out kitchen that could easily be packed away.

Another idea is to maximize the vertical space within the container home. Walls are great for hanging small items such as clothes. Outfits can be placed on hangers, while magnetic boards can be used to hold portable utensils and cutlery. This idea works for people who do not have many belongings, and if you want to commit to a single unit container home, you may want to consider letting some of your belongings go.

The rooftop can be used to create outdoor space. This works well in warm climates or during the summer in cold climates. Reinforcing the roof using a method similar to planting an eco-roof works well. Stairs can be built to gain access to the roof, where you can place outdoor furniture and enjoy the sun. This can be an outdoor lounging area or an outdoor office. Just be careful to avoid falling off the roof. If this is a concern, you can build a barrier, similar to how balconies are built in apartments. Additionally, the rooftop can also be used as storage space for items that are not regularly used.

Home Automation

The second major problem is that shipping container homes are not digital friendly. The significance of this problem depends on the individual needs, because I know a few people who actually use their shipping container home to get away from the busyness of city life. But for some, it has become an integral part of daily life, and if the container home functions as the main residence, it must be adapted to suit the daily needs. Modern surveillance systems for home security rely on wifi and other wireless communication channels to function. Fortunately, there are ways to solve this problem.

Smart homes are becoming a common feature as technology gets more advanced and affordable. If you like the idea of an automated shipping container home you have to go further than using wifi extenders and boosters as previously discussed. Turning down the transmit power also known as TX power for your wifi and connections can help reduce signal attenuation when many devices are connected to the same network. By default, most wireless routers and devices are tuned to their maximum and this is not efficient if there are metal barriers. You can also try to change the frequencies as well as try to locate the antennas in a central location. By changing the frequencies, you may find an optimum signal for your devices. In a shipping container home that retains large portions of the original corrugated steel walls, the best solution for all networked electronic devices remains using a hard wired connection. Before installing home automation and security systems, ask the installer if there are any hardwired options available. While individual devices can be automated, an integrated automation system will give you a complete experience. Usually, items that are automated are electrical appliances, lights, entertainment systems and security systems.

Intelligent Lighting: New home owners do not need to worry about compatibility with existing devices. Your preferences will determine the types of smart lighting systems to choose. For instance, you may prefer lights that dim at a certain time, or lights that switch on while you are away on vacation. The advantage is that in the long run, there are savings on electrical costs, because the lights only turn on when they are required. Regular hardware stores sell different systems that can be set up by a regular person. You can decide on a professionally installed system if you are looking for sophisticated effects, such as a voice controlled intelligent lighting system.

Entertainment Control: Clutter makes small homes look crowded, making the case for minimalism. With multimedia automation, there is no need to keep track of remotes for every gadget you have. Using a control center and mobile applications, entertainment systems can be controlled from anywhere in the house, and outside. You can always make sure that your kids are not watching too much television while you are away if you have an automated multimedia system. Options include models offered by Sentiosec, Control 4, Crestron and Roussound.

Security and Protection: protecting your investment is probably the most important goal of automating your home. Besides using automation to maintain privacy or detecting intruders, you can install systems that detect leakages from gas before a fire breaks out. Virtually anything can be automated if the right equipment is installed. The availability of different types of sensors makes this possible, and an example of sensors are water leak sensors which are used to prevent flooding inside the home.

Tips

Converting a container into a functional space is physically demanding. It also takes a lot of time and tips are handy to save you from biting off more than you can chew. I have added some tips you can use to reduce the workload no matter the size of your build.

- **Make Use of the Community:** Learning is a continuous process and the DIY community is constantly developing hacks. Heading to a community channel on YouTube or other content sharing platforms will give you ideas on the practical parts of your build and help you avoid costly mistakes. Be sure to look around for a demonstration of the building process before you start building.

- **Add Structural Elements Before Cutting**: Even if you build a small home, adding the structural supports and the roof before cutting will guard against some parts of the container collapsing if you exceed the maximums specified in the codes. I started as an amateur too, and I know sometimes mistakes happen with your first build.

- **Outsource as Much as You Can:** Unless you have superb DIY skills and have tools already lying around, outsource part of the work such as the building of your cupboards to reduce the workload. Some hardware stores provide cutting, planing, and sanding services using quality industrial equipment if you purchase your materials with them.

- **Buy Used Tools:** Sometimes buying new tools for a single build does not make financial sense. If you live in the United States, head over to Craigslist and look for used tools. DIYers in the UK and Australia can try Gumtree to find deals that can save money on their build, while those in Canada can try popular sites like Kajiji. You can save even more money by borrowing tools from neighbors and friends. Just remember to return them when you are done.

- **Choose a Sunny Spot in Cold Climates:** Take advantage of the radiant heat from the sun to warm up your house naturally. You can also paint your container home with a dark non-reflective color, so that this heat is not lost quickly at night. Remember elementary school science—dark and dull surfaces absorb and trap heat better than light and shiny surfaces.

- **Save on Climate Control Costs:** Consider a design that lets you separate the containers with a gap of around six feet. This will help you with better air circulation. If possible, put a bag of cat litter at both ends of the container. Open the bag so that the litter can absorb moisture.

FAQ

- **Is a shipping container home the right choice for me?**

  Not everyone buys into the idea of living in a shipping container home. You can try living in a shipping container home by renting one for a couple of months. There are so many places where you can rent a container home temporarily. You can even find one on Airbnb. In Squirrel Park, Oklahoma for example, you can find a unit to rent for $2,000 per month. The contracts can be short term or long term.

- **Shipping containers homes are allowed in my area, but I don't want my home to stand out. What can I do?**

  It's common to see shipping container homes decorated with cladding and wood in the urban areas and city centers. Doing this introduces another question however. Is the climate suitable for exterior covering and will the insulation be placed on the exterior? Once you figure this out, you can choose the right option to cover your shipping container home.

- **I want to save on the building costs, and double glazed windows are expensive. What can I do?**

  Single pane windows lose significant heat compared to an insulated wall of equal size. If you cannot afford a double pane glass for your windows, consider smaller windows. You will have a smaller surface area through which heat can be lost. Consider installing insulating drapes over your windows.

- **There are many insulation options. How can I get a general idea on how to insulate my container home?**

  The rule of thumb is that hot climates do not require slab insulation, low wall insulation, and high ceiling attic insulation. Mild regions that do not have high cooling and heating costs do not need to achieve high R-values. If you pay a fortune for cooling and heating, you will need high levels of insulation all around the house.

- **Are shipping container homes pet friendly?**

  Yes. Shipping container homes are safe for you to live in, meaning they can also be safe for your pets. The way you design your home will determine if it is pet friendly or otherwise. You can install a doggie door just like you would in a traditional house, but you should make sure you have taken the recommended steps to keep temperatures inside the container regulated.

- **I live in a flood prone area, can I build a shipping container home there?**

  All homes get their stability from the foundation. If you worry that your home will flood, you can ask a structural engineer about how you can build the foundation. Pier foundations give you the option of raising your container home above the regular flood levels, but there are limits to the height of the concrete pier. Another way to flood proof your home is to consider a multi-story build that does not modify the base container's doors. The original doors of a shipping container are water tight, and you can cut and install a window section on them while preserving the wall and seals.

- **Can a container home survive a hurricane?**

    Often, I get asked if a shipping container home can survive natural disasters such as tornadoes and hurricanes. The greatest advantage shipping container homes have over traditional houses is their mass per square foot. Unless a super tornado such as the one depicted in the movie *Man of Steel* strikes, a shipping container home should be expected to survive a number of disasters if precautions are taken. Typically, hurricanes create powerful winds that are accompanied by rain, and potential floods. Unmodified shipping containers are watertight and impenetrable by flying objects because of the tight seal and thick steel walls.

    When building a shipping container home in a disaster prone area, the pre-purchase inspection stage is even more critical. If the seals are damaged, water can leak into the house under flooding conditions. Modifications also introduce weak links such as glass doors and windows, so careful considerations are needed for your house to survive natural disasters. The key is to secure the container and reinforce vulnerable areas like glass windows. Timber and brick houses get damaged when the violent winds cause the structure to disintegrate. Shipping containers are designed to withstand rough marine conditions, and are naturally expected to fare better than traditional houses. Powerful hurricanes can toss an unsecured shipping container around, and a shipping container home will need to be adequately anchored to the foundation to avoid being tossed around in severe wind conditions.

    Using pylons attached to a strong foundation is a great way to provide additional stability. Properly anchored shipping containers can withstand winds greater than the maximum speed of a Category Five hurricane, and your container home will be able to withstand a hurricane. Installing hurricane proof windows will enhance the protection that the robust steel structure offers.

- **Can I get insurance?**

    Depending on your location, some insurance companies do provide cover for shipping container homes. Usually, your home receives protection from certain perils such as fire, hail, aircraft accidents, vandalism (general and from riots) as well as explosions. However, it will be difficult to get insurance for things like mold, earthquakes, demolition by authorities, vandalism, or if there is no one living on the premises for more than 60 days. Check with your insurance company for a more comprehensive list.

- **Can a shipping container home explode if there is a gas leak?**

    Ventilation is a must in a shipping container home, particularly if you are going to be keeping flammable materials such as propane gas for cooking, which is highly flammable. If there is no ventilation and the gas ignites, the container may explode. Although this has not been recorded in a residential container home, there have been several cases where a tightly sealed shipping container exploded when flammable gas ignited. If you don't want to install vents, place your windows high up and on opposite ends. They will act as vents when open.

- **Do shipping container homes have good resale value?**

    Shipping container homes are becoming popular. Traditional houses still have a real estate value that is higher than shipping container homes, but compared to RVs and trailer houses, shipping container homes are considered more permanent. Besides, the tiny house movement continues to grow, and you can expect to get real value from your shipping container home if you decide to sell it. You may find it difficult to sell container homes that are temporary because prospective buyers may want the house to meet the codes of their local authority.

- **Besides building a container home, what else can I do with a used shipping container?**

Not all container conversions become homes. Some companies have modelled their business around shipping containers. The major incentive is since they are easy to customize and relatively cheap to acquire, converting shipping containers is an affordable way to own the buildings critical to their operations. Small chains have also discovered that using shipping container homes as business premises also associates their brands with sustainability. Most owners cite the ability to move when the location does not meet the expectation as the greatest advantage. They can simply move to test a new location, without breaching rental agreements. Other uses include emergency shelters, storage facilities, and workshops.

CONCLUSION

Shipping container homes are indeed the ultimate upcycling project for alternative housing. Their abundance and unfortunate disposal have created environmental problems, and the costs to recycle the metal consumes a lot of energy. Climate change is a big concern, and reducing the carbon footprint is a priority that everyone must take seriously. It's clear that shipping containers will continue to be manufactured for the transport industry, because global trade relies on this structure to move the goods we need. Reusing a shipping container is clearly the best way to offset their carbon footprint. This makes sense when used shipping containers are used to build the home.

There are other advantages to building a shipping container home besides benefits to the environment. Their modular structure makes them unbeatable as customizable and scalable housing units that are worth investing in. In a world that is increasingly experiencing natural disasters such as hurricanes, having a sturdy and robust home is comforting. Apart from this, a shipping container home allows you to be part of the build and DIY builds help you develop skills you never thought you had. In my case, building shipping container homes with the help of my family and friends was the greatest reward.

This does not mean that shipping container homes do not have challenges. While they are modular, they are also heavy. Moving them is not easy. You will need a truck to deliver any shipping containers you purchase, and the options available to you depend on the distance, among other factors. Shipping container homes also require extensive modifications for you to live comfortably. Since the material is made of corten steel, problems such as condensation and unbearable temperatures are unique to shipping container homes. However, as the saying goes, where there is a will, there is a way and many enthusiasts, designers, engineers and architects have worked so tirelessly to identify how to optimize living conditions in shipping container homes built in different climates. The variety of eco-friendly and sustainable products meant for insulating the house is a sure sign that shipping container houses are becoming widely accepted.

Other challenges include getting connected while living in a shipping container home. Our modern society relies on the internet and not having a reliable connection can be a deterrent to people thinking about building a shipping container home. Fortunately there are solutions to this, and implementing them will require flexibility on the prospective shipping container home occupant. Getting a wired connection is the most effective solution to resolve the connectivity problems. This works well in urban areas where fiber broadband can easily be accessed. Container homes located off-grid can consider a satellite connection together with a router that allows an ethernet connection as a workaround to the effect of the metal walls on the signal's strength.

The possibilities with shipping container homes are endless. If you want to build your house off-grid, shipping containers are the ideal construction component because they can be easily transported. In part, climate change and the green movement has influenced this rising trend of shipping container houses. The increase in popularity has led to states and local authorities across the world developing regulations for shipping container buildings. To know if cargotecture is allowed in your region, contact the local authority before you decide to commit. This is the most important lesson that you must take away from this book.

Other than this, there are other critical steps you must take to build your shipping container home. Preparation is key, and it is important to spend some time planning for your project. Knowing how much you are willing to spend will determine the type of shipping container you will buy, the quantity, and ultimately the size of your home. Once you have a budget, speak to an architect or structural engineer to know the possibilities and the limitations of your build. This way, you will be able to match your dream, the law, and professional opinion to create a design that works. Planning your project before you start will guarantee your success and help you avoid expensive mistakes. Fortunately, the lessons provided in this book are based on the lessons I have learned over the years.

While the true spirit of building shipping container homes is the potential for DIY building, another lesson that I hope resonates with you is to leave dangerous activities to qualified personnel. The installation of electricity is one example. Of course, if you are technically competent, you can do the basic tasks such as wiring or even making the connections to the distribution board. But connecting to the main power line is something best left to certified electricians. You may not get the installation passed if the connections are made by uncertified persons. By following the steps detailed in this book, you will minimize your mistakes, and know when to seek professional help.

If you are not sure whether living in a shipping container home will suit your lifestyle, renting is a good place to start. In some neighborhoods, shipping container homes have become the main building theme, and if you look around, you might be able to find a perfect example of what you are looking for. Airbnb is a good starting point for short stays, but you can also find long term rental options that can suit your budget. On the high end, it is not uncommon to find owners of shipping container homes asking for as much as $2,000 per month in rentals.

Top Shipping Container Home Mistakes to Avoid

Building a shipping container home is a very detailed process, and mistakes are bound to happen. Some mistakes are more forgiving than others, and you must avoid mistakes that will make your life unbearable, are expensive to fix, or land you in trouble with the law. Here are the top mistakes to avoid when building a shipping container home.

Purchasing containers that are damaged: If the price is too good to be true, it probably is. Of course the idea is to buy used containers, but if you find a container that is cheaper than usual, you must be careful. This is usually the case with containers that are too old. What you save on the initial price will be spent on making repairs to restore its condition. In the end, you could end up paying more than if you had bought a more expensive container that is in good condition.

Building the foundation after the containers have arrived: This is a common mistake that many DIY builders make. Repositioning the container will not be easy without heavy lifting equipment, and you may need to spend extra financial resources to rent the equipment again.

Selecting the wrong insulation material: Most DIYers accidentally pick the wrong insulating material because they fail to consider the conditions that their home will be exposed to. Sometimes, cost also plays a role in the decision, leading to shortcuts. Choosing the wrong insulation will make you regret investing in a shipping container home. You may be able to get away with poor insulation in a traditional home, because of the insulating effect of materials used to build ordinary houses, but the container's corrugated walls are excellent conductors, and heat is easily transferred from a source to the other side.

Biting off more than you can chew: Building a shipping container home requires a considerable amount of labor and skill. Many people make the mistake of trying to build their first home without acquiring the basic skills needed to complete the project. It is a good idea to learn skills like woodworking and welding, so that the final project is visually appealing. Poor workmanship and cutting corners is the main reason some people end up unsatisfied with their builds. The costs to build a shipping container house can escalate very quickly if you live in cold climates or in a highly regulated state. Having the ability to complete some parts of the build yourself will save you on labor, but you need to know your limits. The community around you is a good place to learn. The internet has many resources that you can find to reinforce what you have learned in this book. Other than this, your family and friends can help you out with some power tools required for single unit container builds. I do not recommend trying to convert more than two shipping containers the first time if you have no DIY skills.

Too much modification: The codes specify the portions that may be cut for a good reason. Knowing that a shipping container is a robust structure can be misleading. The walls and roof have no structural properties and excessive cutting makes the resulting structure unstable which may collapse. I have seen many shipping container home builds fail. Besides being a waste of financial resources, a failed shipping container structure risks damaging property within its vicinity and can possibly lead to loss of life if parts of the structure fall. This risk is higher in multi-story container buildings.

Ignoring building codes and zoning laws: Surprisingly, this happens often and if done in a zoned area, the fines can be steep. DIYers who have trouble interpreting the codes should consider running their idea by a building officer. You can usually do this at no cost, which will allow you to get some advice without having to pay a structural engineer. Although, ultimately, the building officer may require an engineer's stamp of approval on your plans before you can proceed. Other important legal issues include the safety of contractors or assistants helping with the building process. It is important that you keep safety in mind when converting your shipping container home. Products like insulation spray can be toxic, and using power tools requires extreme care. Safety at work is a concept that is universal, and in some states, ignoring safe work makes you liable to prosecution.

Thinking that building a container home is cheap: Shipping container houses are generally less expensive to build than traditional houses. This does not mean they are cheap to build. In some cases, the final cost can exceed the cost of a traditional house because a number of factors affect the total cost of building a shipping container home. Factors such as distance, condition of shipping containers, and the design contribute to the cost of building the home. Planning a project before making a commitment is the only way to make sure that the financial resources available are sufficient to complete the project.

Other Uses of Shipping Containers

The use of shipping containers as building components is not limited to housing. Coffee shops, clothing shops and restaurants are some examples of businesses that have switched to modular buildings in an attempt to make their operations more sustainable. If the location no longer meets the business objectives of a company, using shipping containers makes relocation a breeze. In the long-run, companies save on rental costs because they can own the premises which form the backbone of their operations.

You may need to ask yourself how you can make shipping containers part of your life. In this book, we have discussed a number of designs and functions, but the possibilities are endless. I am certain that this book has inspired you to think sustainably and approach housing from an eco-friendly perspective. I am confident that you will take the concepts presented to heart, and wish you success on your cargotecture journey. Please consider giving an honest review of the book if you enjoyed it and found it informative.

REFERENCES

1300Sparebox. (2021). *Ten steps to build a shipping container home.* https://1300sparebox.com.au/ten-steps-build-shipping-container-home/.

American Geo Services. (n.d.). *Foundation design for shipping container homes.* http://americangeoservices.com/foundation-design-for-shipping-container-homes.html.

Ameriside. (September 03, 2020). *Pros and cons of elastomeric paint.* https://www.ameriside.com/pros-and-cons-of-elastomeric-paint/.

Architecture Lab. (November 11, 2020). *7 Best container home design software options.*

Ataei, M. (2019). *Design of a two story ISO shipping container building.*

Barunga West District Council. (2020). *Shipping Container Homes.* https://www.barungawest.sa.gov.au/__data/assets/pdf_file/0029/228377/Shipping-Container-Policy-2016V1.pdf.

BC Hydro Power Smart. (n.d.). Charges & fees for connections. https://app.bchydro.com/accounts-billing/electrical-connections/charges-fees.html.

Bison Jacks. (2021). *Weigh containers yourself with C-Jacks. On the ground or on the chassis.*

Boris, J. (June 03, 2021). *Floor insulation and moisture concerns in hot climates, vapour barrier sandwich.* Green Building Advisor. https://www.greenbuildingadvisor.com/question/floor-insulation-and-moisture-concerns-in-hot-climates

Bradnams. (n.d.). *5 Benefits of double glazing windows and doors.* https://www.bradnams.com.au/benefits-of-double-glazing-windows/

Brett, J. (2021). What is a smart shipping container home and why are we building one? Creation Station. https://www.creationstation.build/blog/what-is-a-smart-home-and-why-are-we-building-one.

Budget Shipping Containers. (September 03, 2019). *Painting your own shipping container.* https://www.budgetshippingcontainers.co.uk/info/painting-your-own-shipping-container/?cn-reloaded=1

Cad Details. (July 02, 2021). *How should I protect my shipping container home from rust?* https://caddetailsblog.com/post/how-should-i-protect-my-shipping-container-home-from-rust.

Cepods. (n.d.). *Frequently asked questions.* https://www.cepods.com/faqs.

City of Aberdeen. (2019). Aberdeen City Code. Municode. https://library.municode.com/sd/aberdeen/codes/code_of_ordinances?nodeId=ABCO.

Container Addict. (n.d.). *How much does it cost to move a shipping container?* https://containeraddict.com/moving-container-cost/#:~:text=Generally%2C%20moving%20containers%20across%20the,to%20four%20dollars%20per%20mile

Container Container. (n.d.). *Shipping container dimensions.* https://containercontainer.com/shipping-container-dimensions/

Container Homes. (n.d.). *How to paint a shipping container home.* https://containerhomes.net/learning-center/how-to-center/how-to-paint-a-shipping-container-home/.

Container Homes. (n.d.). *Installing a septic tank for a container home.* https://containerhomes.net/learning-center/how-to-center/installing-a-septic-tank-for-a-container-home/

Container One. (March 11, 2021). *Keeping your shipping container cool in the summer.* https://containerone.net/blogs/news/keeping-your-shipping-container-cool-in-the-summer.

Container One. (April 07, 2020). *How to build a shipping container cabin: a step-by-step guide.* https://containerone.net/blogs/news/how-to-build-a-shipping-container-cabin.

Coop, L. (April 6, 2021). *Understanding the UK laws of a tiny house.* Tiny Housing Co. https://www.thetinyhousing.co/blog/understanding-the-uk-laws-of-a-tiny-house.

Container One. (February 01, 2021). *How to insulate a shipping container - 5 commonly used methods.* https://containerone.net/blogs/news/how-to-insulate-a-shipping-container-5-commonly-used-methods.

Discover Containers. (November 24, 2020). *Best types of shipping container insulation.* https://www.discovercontainers.com/5-methods-to-insulate-your-shipping-container-home/.

Discover Containers. (June 01, 2021). *Five must have tools for a container home building project.* https://www.discovercontainers.com/tools-needed-to-build-a-shipping-container-home/.

Discover Containers. (June 01, 2021). *How to choose the right shipping containers.* https://www.discovercontainers.com/complete-guide-to-buying-shipping-containers/.

Discover Containers. (December 20, 2019). *How should you ventilate your shipping container building?* https://www.discovercontainers.com/how-should-you-ventilate-your-shipping-container-home/.

Discover Containers. (December 20, 2019). *How to select a roof for your shipping container building.* https://www.discovercontainers.com/how-to-fit-a-roof-onto-your-shipping-container/.

Discover Containers. (March 24, 2021). *How to stop container condensation.* https://www.discovercontainers.com/container-condensation-prevention/.

Discover Containers. (December 29, 2019). *Rust and Corrosion In Shipping Container Homes.* https://www.discovercontainers.com/shipping-container-home-rust-and-corrosion-treatment/.

Discover Containers. (n.d.). *Shipping container dimensions and sizes.* https://www.discovercontainers.com/shipping-container-dimensions/.

Discover Containers. (December 21, 2019). *Shipping container flooring and pesticides.* https://www.discovercontainers.com/should-you-remove-the-plywood-floors-in-your-shipping-containers/

Discover Containers. (July 30, 2021). *Shipping container accessory attachments.* https://www.discovercontainers.com/container-accessory-attachments/.

Discover Containers. (April 8, 2021). *Shipping container site preparation.* https://www.discovercontainers.com/shipping-container-site-preparation/.

Discover Containers. (October 01, 2020). *Shipping container home foundations 101.* https://www.discovercontainers.com/shipping-container-home-foundation-types/.

Discover Containers. (November 24, 2020). *Should you build with refrigerated shipping containers?* https://www.discovercontainers.com/should-you-use-a-refrigerated-shipping-container-for-your-container-home/.

Discover Container. (November 4, 2020). *The best types of shipping container insulation.* https://www.discovercontainers.com/5-methods-to-insulate-your-shipping-container-home/.

Domino Clamps. (2021). *Description.* https://dominoclamps.com/.

Earth911. (April 14, 2020). *Earth Day: 23 of the greatest environmental quotes.* https://earth911.com/inspire/earth-day-23-quotes/.

Elderedge, B. (September 27, 2016). *Case study: How to install a green roof on a private home.* Curbed. https://archive.curbed.com/2016/9/27/12830392/green-roof-installation-design-private-home.

Energy Australia. (2021). Other fees and charges. https://www.energyaustralia.com.au/home/help-and-support/faqs/other-fees-and-charges.

Energy Information Administration. (December 15, 2020). *How much carbon dioxide is produced per kiloWatthour of U.S. electricity generation?* https://www.eia.gov/tools/faqs/faq.php?id=74&t=11.

Five Star Painting. (September 01, 2020). *How to paint shiplap.* https://www.fivestarpainting.com/blog/2020/september/how-to-paint-shiplap/.

Fortis BC. (2021). Getting natural gas - it's easier than you think. https://www.fortisbc.com/services/natural-gas-services/getting-natural-gas-its-easier-than-you-think

Gateway Containers. (2020). *Gett off-grid with a shipping container home.* https://www.gatewaycontainersales.com.au/get-off-grid-with-a-shipping-container-home/.

Gateway Containers. (2020). *Shipping container home prices: how much do container homes cost to build?* https://gatewaycontainersales.com.au/shipping-container-home-prices-how-much-do-container-homes-cost/.

Green Roof Guide. (February 4, 2021). *5 Best green roof filter layers.* https://www.greenroofguide.com/green-roofs/best-filter-layers/#:~:text=A%20green%20roof%20filter%20layer%20prevents%20finer%20particles%20of%20growing,your%20living%20roof's%20drainage%20system.

Green Roof Solutions. (n.d.). *Drainage.* https://www.greenroofsolutions.com/products/green-roof/extensive-intensive-semi-intensive/drainage/

Hand, J. (January 19, 2018). *Expert advice: The enduring appeal of shiplap.* Remodelista. https://www.remodelista.com/posts/expert-advice-shiplap/

Harbour, S. (September 7, 2021). *Off grid toilets: which one do you want for your home.* Off Grid Life. https://www.anoffgridlife.com/off-grid-toilets/.

Harnett, C. (February 28, 2018). *Shipping containers and propane tanks are an explosive mix.* Times Colonist. https://www.timescolonist.com/business/shipping-containers-and-propane-tanks-are-an-explosive-mix-1.23186881.

Haspod. (January 4, 2019). *Safe use of power tools (and hazards to watch out for).* https://www.haspod.com/blog/construction/safe-use-power-tools.

Holladay, M. (October 18, 2019). *Insulating a wood-framed floor assembly.* Green Building Advisor. https://greenbuildingadvisor.com/article/insulating-a-wood-framed-floor-assembly

House Energy. (n.d.). *Insulation levels for attics, walls, floors and basements in cold, mixed and hot climates.* https://www.house-energy.com/Insulation/Insulation-Climate-Zone.htm

I Container Home. (n.d.). *Costs and benefits of 40' high cube vs 40' standard shipping container.* https://icontainerhome.com/cost-and-benefits-of-40high-cube-vs-40-standard-shipping-container/#:~:text=A%2040ft.,a%20standard%20one%20for%20%242%2C000.

I Container Home. (n.d.). *Electrical wiring of shipping container home.* https://icontainerhome.com/electrical-wiring-of-shipping-container-home/.

I Container Home. (2020). *Grounding and earthing of shipping container home.* https://icontainerhome.com/grounding-and-earthing-of-shipping-container-home/.

ICC Digital Codes. (2020). *New provisions for shipping containers in the 2021 IBC.* https://codes.iccsafe.org/content/ICCG52019/appendix-3-new-provisions-for-shipping-containers-in-the-2021-ibc-to-be-published-in-2020-.

InSoFast. (n.d.). *How to frame out a shipping container home.* https://www.insofast.com/lc/how-frame-out-shipping-container-home.html.

Jessica, P. (April 3, 2021). *Off the Grid: The best way to cut through steel shipping containers.* The Fabricator. https://www.thefabricator.com/thefabricator/blog/cuttingweldprep/off-the-grid-the-best-way-to-cut-through-steel-shipping-containers.

Johnson, M. (2020). *Off grid internet: 6 Ways to get internet access when living off the grid.* Down To Earth Homesteaders. https://downtoearthhomesteaders.com/6-ways-to-get-internet-access-when-living-off-grid/

Lane, L. (n.d.). *How do you put a door and window in a shipping container?* Live In A Container. https://liveinacontainer.com/how-do-you-put-a-door-and-window-in-a-shipping-container/.

Masterclass. (November 8, 2020). *Shipping container homes: understanding the pros and cons.* https://www.masterclass.com/articles/shipping-container-homes-understanding-the-pros-and-cons.

Melton, K & Todtenhagen, C. (June 10, 2020). *Spray foam: open-cell vs closed cell.* JM. https://www.jm.com/en/blog/2020/june/spray-foam--open-cell-vs--closed-cell/

Mig Welding. (n.d.). *Welding corten steel.* https://www.mig-welding.co.uk/corten.htm.

Miller Welds. (n.d.). *Factors for selecting the right stick electrode.* https://www.millerwelds.com/resources/article-library/factors-for-selecting-the-right-stick-electrode.

ModuGo. (2021). *Shipping container site preparation guide: do these things to make delivery easy.* https://modugo.com/blog/shipping-container-site-preparation-guide-do-these-things-to-make-delivery-easy/.

Morin, M. (November 20, 2019). *Choose the best windows for a shipping container structure.* Falcon Structures. https://www.falconstructures.com/blog/best-windows-for-shipping-container.

Morin, M. (September 15, 2021). *How the structural strength of shipping containers stands up to severe weather.* Falcon Structures. https://www.falconstructures.com/blog/shipping-container-structural-strength.

Morin, M. (August 12, 2020). *5 Shipping container floor options to ensure durability.* Falcon Structures. https://www.falconstructures.com/blog/shipping-container-flooring.

Morin, M. (July 28, 2021). *Shipping container air conditioning, heating, and ventilation.* Falcon Structures. https://www.falconstructures.com/blog/shipping-container-heating-cooling.

National Park Service. (n.d.). *What is a green roof?* U.S. Department of the Interior. https://www.nps.gov/tps/sustainability/new-technology/green-roofs/define.htm

New South Wales Government. (n.d.). *Becoming an owner-builder.* NSWG. https://www.fairtrading.nsw.gov.au/housing-and-property/building-and-renovating/becoming-an-owner-builder.

OEMServ. (n.d.). *Shipping container - capacity and weights.* https://www.oemserv.com/shipping-information.html#:~:text=The%20side%20walls%20of%20shipping,50mm%20from%20the%20external%20dimensions.

Off Grid World. (July 9, 2020). *8 Factors to keep in mind when insulating a shipping container home.* https://offgridworld.com/8-factors-to-keep-in-mind-when-insulating-a-shipping-container-home/.

O'Keefe, C. (July 17, 2020). *Cost of spray foam insulation.* Home Advisor. https://homeadvisor.com/cost/insulation/install-spray-foam-insulation/.

Okelo, A. (August 21, 2019). *The different types of interior walls in a shipping container.* Owlcation. https://owlcation.com/humanities/The-Different-Types-of-Interior-Walls-in-a-Shipping-Container.

PamblanCo Paint. (July 20, 2020). *How do you prepare drywall for painting?* https://www.pamblancopainting.com/how-do-you-prepare-drywall-for-painting/.

Pedraza, R. (September 18, 2019). *How to clean the insides of a shipping container.* Mobile Modular. https://blog.mobilemodularcontainers.com/how-clean-insides-shipping-container.

Prefab Review. (May 02, 2019). *Best prefab shipping container home manufacturers and builders.* https://www.prefabreview.com/blog/best-prefab-shipping-container-home-manufacturers-and-builders.

Purios. (n.d.). *Green-roof installation - what do you use to insulate an extensive roof?* https://purios.com/en/blog/green-roof-insulation-what-do-you-use-to-insulate-an-extensive-roof

Quickfit (n.d.). *Shipping container bridge* clamp. https://www.quickfitcontaineraccessories.co.uk/shop/bridge-clamps/shipping-container-bridge-clamp/.

Raven, B. (January 30, 2019). *ADSL vs Fibre broadband: what do they mean and which do I need?* Tech Radar. https://www.techradar.com/broadband/adsl-vs-fibre-broadband.

Rivas, L.R. (July 22, 2021). *Pros and cons of shipping container homes.* MYSA.

Roberts, T. (April 24, 2018). *4 ways to insulate a container home.* Rise. https://www.buildwithrise.com/stories/4-ways-to-insulate-a-container-home.

Saltzman, M. (November 25, 2017). *Light up your house with LEDs, and other tips to slash your electric bill.* USA Today. https://www.usatoday.com/story/tech/columnist/saltzman/2017/11/25/light-up-your-house-leds-and-other-energy-saving-tips/894537001/.

Sanguir, J. (june 16, 2019). *The importance of using twist lock stacking pins on shipping containers.* Quickfit. https://www.quickfitcontaineraccessories.co.uk/twistlock-stacking-pins/

Schwartz, D.M. (2020). *Best alternative off grid toilets - no septic.* Off Grid Permaculture. https://offgridpermaculture.com/Water_Systems/Best_Alternative_Off_Grid_Toilets___No_Septic_.html.

Secure. (April 12, 2021). *Do you need a permit for shipping containers?* SCS. https://www.securecontainer.ca/need-permit-shipping-containers/.

Semper Green. (n.d.). *Does a green roof have an insulating effect?* https://www.sempergreen.com/en/solutions/green-roofs/frequently-asked-questions-green-roof/green-roof-insulation

Setherton, G. n.d.). *Green roof construction - how to guide.* Permagard. https://www.permagard.co.uk/advice/green-roof-construction.

SharpLaunch. (n.d.). *Top 11 green building certifications that can increase your property's marketability.* https://www.sharplaunch.com/blog/green-building-certifications/.

S Jones Containers. (n.d.). *Shipping container homes UK Planning Permission regulations.* https://www.sjonescontainers.co.uk/containerpedia/shipping-container-homes-uk-planning-permission-regulations/.

S Jones Containers. (n.d.). *What cleaning products are safe to use on a shipping container?* https://www.sjonescontainers.co.uk/containerpedia/what-cleaning-products-are-safe-to-use-on-a-shipping-container/.

Seinecker. (2012). *Technical specification for a typical 40'x 8'x 9'6" ISO type steel dry cargo container "high cube".* http://steinecker-container.de/container/Container2/Spez-Container/Spez_high%20cube40.pdf.

Slow The Flow. (July 31, 2019). Green roof on a shipping container. https://slowtheflow.net/green-roof-on-a-shipping-container/.

Taylor, G. (n.d.). *PEX vs. copper: Which pipes are right for my home?* Bob Villa. https://www.bobvila.com/articles/pex-vs-copper/.

The Tiny House. (n.d.). *How to convert a shipping container into a tiny house in 13 steps.* https://www.thetinyhouse.net/how-to-convert-shipping-container-tiny-house/.

Total Materia. (2002). *Welding procedures and the fundamentals of welding.* https://www.totalmateria.com/page.aspx?ID=CheckArticle&site=kts&NM=77.

W&K Container (September 25, 2018). In need of ISO containers? https://www.oceancontainer.com/representative-projects.

Warwick, S. (2021). Underfloor heating – a guide to installation and costs. Real Homes. https://www.realhomes.com/advice/underfloor-heating-your-questions-answered.

Watkins, N. (February 07, 2019). *Cable distance limits.* Show Me Cables. https://www.showmecables.com/blog/post/cable-distance-limits-data.

Weldwire (2021). E7018. http://www.weldwire.net/weld_products/ww7018/.

Welsh, P. (November 8, 2017). *Shipping containers hold up in structures.* Falcon Structures. https://www.falconstructures.com/blog/shipping-container-structural-strength.

Western Power. (n.d.). Standard electricity supply for a single house. https://www.westernpower.com.au/connections/power-supply/new-connections/standard-electricity-supply-for-a-single-house/.

Whitney, C. (November 19, 2019). *The ultimate downsize: Living in a shipping container home.* Howstuffworks. https://science.howstuffworks.com/innovation/repurposed-inventions/live-in-shipping-container.htm.

Young Alfred. (July 21, 2021). *Which states allow shipping container homes?* https://www.youngalfred.com/homeowners-insurance/which-states-allow-shipping-container-homes.

Made in the USA
Las Vegas, NV
10 January 2024

84169879R00072